THE
COMPASS
SOLUTION

A Guide to Winning Your Career
TIM COLE

The Compass Alliance, LLC
11820 Dan Maples Drive, Charlotte, NC 28277   USA

www.thecompassalliance.com

ISBN 978-0-9990571-0-0

Library of Congress Control Number: 2017950361

FIRST EDITION

Printed in the United States of America

This book is dedicated to the many people I encountered on my career journey – and especially those willing to offer guidance and perspective along the way. There are too many to try and name but please know you each had a hand in writing the pages that follow.

It's important I also thank Susan Hart, whose perspective and guidance helped morph a compilation of essays into something much more – as well as take my version of The Compass and make it far better.

Finally, a special thanks to my mom and dad for gifts I did not appreciate until I became a father, to my sons Brandon and David who are each far better equipped for their career story than their old man ever was, and to the little girl I met a long, long time ago who was destined to someday become my wife. Nancy, you've been with me every step of the way. You helped write this great adventure.

C O N T E N T S

PREFACE

One hundred thousand hours.

That's what you should estimate the average journey is going to be when you take your first steps onto the job trail; a hundred thousand hours of your life devoted to forging a career path. Do the math yourself.

On the low end—an average of 50 hours per workweek and 45 weeks per year for 40 years. You start when you're 22, and if you're lucky, you hope you're financially able to wrap by the time you're 62. Forty years of your life. The low number is 90,000 hours. The high end is much, much higher. That 50-hour workweek and the golden retirement at 62 are unlikely for most.

Of course, very few think in those terms when they walk through the door with their dreams for the future. Most of us are hardwired to live and breathe for what happens today. And even fewer take the time to understand the lay of the land beyond their immediate job description. I didn't.

Go online today and you will be able to find primers for everything from enduring lightning strikes to navigating zombie apocalypses. But few to none that speak to where most of us devote such a large part of our lives.

This book does. It's the one I wish someone had pushed into my hands the day I walked off my college campus—before I removed the cap and gown, before I put on my first dress shirt, before I walked into my first meeting, and before I ever opened my mouth.

I wish I had it when I encountered my first great career obstacle or when I struggled to endure a supervisor I was convinced was going to ruin my life. It would have saved me a lot of anxious moments and offered me perspective that was not always easy to find.

Maybe this book is for you. It is a candid recounting of lessons learned by one person who navigated the better part of three-plus decades in one of the most highly competitive industries in the world—a diary filled with personal life lessons and journal entries that I've taken the time to balance with proven theory. It is the guidebook that could make more difference in your professional life than any resource you will ever read.

My credentials: I spent all that time with one company, through two-dozen plus restructures and downsizings. And when I say one company, I should point out that included five mergers resulting in six different cultures. Six restarts—six new beginnings. The average company tenure in the corporate world is slightly above four years, which means I managed to beat that ninefold.

The firm I went to work for generated $80 million in sales per year. Before I left, the little portion of the business I personally ran did slightly less than a half of a billion by itself.

I became part of one of the most dramatic company ascensions in the health-care industry, complete with the ebb and flow associated with product pipelines and changing market dynamics. In retrospect, my survival over the course of that many years had about as much probability as winning the lottery on consecutive weeks.

Hold the applause. I was very lucky.

The reality is I made it because I learned a few things along the way that began to increase my chances for survival—lessons I wish someone might have offered me free-of-charge when my journey began.

The pages that follow speak to challenges that are universal to anyone in the corporate world, but they are equally transferrable to almost any field of endeavor. I talk corporate throughout this book because I know corporate. I believe the insights offered here could dramatically change your professional life—regardless of what your field of work happens to be.

My goal is not to prepare you to invest a lifetime with one company—or even one industry. It's to offer lessons that make certain you have a sustainable and successful career. There is a big difference.

Unlike some books that might attempt to offer similar lessons, I didn't write this from the perspective of a chief executive officer, an outside consultant, or a training expert. I have taken the journey myself—from entry level to senior executive. The industry I chose was and is among the most volatile in the world. My pedigree is forged from being one of the few who managed to emerge unscathed and strong on the other side. The path I describe is battle-tested. I know—I walked it.

If you're reading this, my guess is you have either embarked on or are preparing your own adventure, and for many, that is in the world of corporate.

And let's get something out of the way now. A great many don't think of their jobs as *"corporate."* They don't work on Wall Street and they never walk into a high-rise or commute into the city. For the purposes of this book, corporate is simply intended to describe a group of individuals charged with delivering a product that ensures that organization is sustainable. For most businesses, that product translates to profitability. This book is not limited to blue suits. If you plan to work in order to earn a living there is value in what you are about to read.

Imagine this book to be the personal diary left behind from someone who walked the trail before you. Every chapter and every word is based on my experiences.

I wrote this for three distinct groups of people:

- Those contemplating a career but lacking the savvy to properly understand and navigate that new world (almost everyone walking off a college campus, or exiting military service, or reconsidering their vocational choices).

- Those already in a career and struggling to find their way—which includes over 50 percent of the workforce in the United States alone.

- The leaders who can influence and build the cultures that allow dedicated employees to thrive.

Your career is anything but a four-letter word—at least for those who understand how to navigate it. Like any field, there are markers that will allow you to plot a course. I can help you find them.

Not too long ago I sat down to talk with an employee struggling to cope with a company restructure, frightened by the prospect that her job might end. When she heard my story she was dumbstruck. *"How,"* she asked, *"could anyone manage to last through all of that?"*

I laughed but then began to think about that comment—a lot. The book you're reading now began with the question: *"If I could go back in time, what's the advice I would want to whisper in my own ear?"*

My answer is in the pages that follow.

INTRODUCTION

This land is far different from the world you dreamed it would be.

The terrain is hard and unforgiving. The tribes that inhabit the neighboring countryside are rumored to be cannibals. Last night, two members of your team didn't make it back to camp. Your chief didn't mention them but everyone knew they are lost. Your group divided the missing teammates' provisions at the campfire, but no one has spoken of them since.

You check the small pouch you carry with you and find the last morsels of food. You didn't sleep last night—only tossed about on your bedroll and waited for the dawn. You look at the other members of your party now as the first strains of sunlight filter through the trees and wonder again why you came here.

Muscle fatigue has given way to a greater exhaustion.

It wasn't supposed to be like this, was it?

You hear someone muttering that the trail only gets tougher from here and you turn to gaze at the mountain that lies ahead.

"What trail?" you ask yourself.

You fear falling behind. You lag behind here and chances are good someone else will get your place. They say there are hundreds back there waiting for you to stumble.

Someone should have told you all of this.

Shouldn't they?

Your chief is barking orders about the mountain ahead but the words seem slurred and wrapped in a haze of hot, thick air. You pull your side pouch on and wish again you had thought to refill your canteen when you crossed that stream yesterday. Somewhere up ahead there must be a path you tell yourself. You watch a few others start to wander to their right, and so you fall in behind them. Better to follow someone—even if it's the wrong way—than to be left behind.

And so, a new day for a great many in the corporate world gets underway. The metaphorical license I use here is exaggerated—to a degree—but not quite as much as many would want to believe.

Those feelings of uncertainty are very real for most. You've entered a land driven by productivity and earnings—and trust me when I say the cannibals that devour the weak are out there.

Most of us start our climbs without a great degree of guidance beyond that provided by our assigned chief—and certainly without any sense of direction on a larger scale. We build our own—or we become one of the lost.

I easily could have become one of the wanderers. I accepted a job offer all those years ago because of base pay and benefits. I had no real vision and certainly no counsel. With no map and no mentor I contented myself with making the next step. When I saw others on the trail, I was inclined to fall in behind. There was a mountain to be climbed.

Until I began to realize there were signs out there that could guide me. And like the survivalist in the natural world, I began to develop instincts that changed me. I had to stumble a few times, but I began to learn.

This book offers you the unvarnished truth around what I've learned. Some of it will seem intuitive. Some of it you may disagree with, and that's OK. But these are the practical lessons from my journey—the personal log that began when I first contemplated the mountain.

This is not a book on theory. It is focused on function and application. To that end, I've divided it into two parts. The first section I call the Compass. Remember, no one hands you a map when you embark on your career. But you can form a sense of direction from the very first day. Consider this section the survival foundation that most struggle to figure out. If they don't, they remained locked in their own version of a perpetual career purgatory. A great many invest their professional lives there.

You don't have to.

Apply the ideas and principles outlined in this portion of the book and you will enjoy advantages most of your peers will never find. You'll be able to seek shelter and you will learn how to effectively "feed yourself" and your career.

The Compass will introduce you to four Cardinal Points essential to that survival. Each took me years to truly comprehend and embrace. They are:

- Personal Accountability
- People
- Process
- Perspective

The lodestar for your compass—Personal Accountability—will become your navigational constant. You will learn to count on it, plan around it, and optimize what it offers you for the rest of your career—or you will abdicate that responsibility and effectively ride the winds.

The other three points of the compass represent either opportunities or obstacles depending on your ability to master the subtleties each offer. Ignore them at your own peril. I watched each drive careers—and sometimes effectively end careers.

The 4 Ps are focused on survival. The short chapters that support each offer foundational points that are then built on over the course of the book—made simple and executable. You'll note that I end each chapter with a Straight Talk summary. Why? Because your time is valuable. I'm not going to pound you with verbiage. I'll share stories, offer experiences, give you the central idea, and then move on.

But when you first contemplated a career you did so with dreams of a better life—not simply subsisting.

Which brings us to the second section—the Key Chain. This is where we introduce you to three Keys that can truly accelerate your career. The chapters that support each offer insight into core competencies that separate the successful from the masses.

These Keys are remarkably simple—and yet I seldom saw them fully optimized over the course of my career. They are:

- Leadership
- Communication
- Learning

Sounds pretty simple doesn't it? How many books have you read on just the subject of leadership alone? And yet every year millions of employees see their careers stall—or their path become terribly clouded.

The value of each of the chapters that support the Keys and the "why" behind this book is simple—there is a big difference between principle and practice in this world. Get used to it. At least some of those theories you discussed in college or carried with you from past experiences may or may not ever become practical reality out here where the game is played.

I write this book as someone who climbed the mountain ahead of you—and experienced the same challenges as you. I condensed the Keys into just three for a reason. These were the ones that were the difference makers. I watched those who mastered them enjoy longevity and success. I watched even more who never understood their intricacies, and continued to stumble until they began to fall. You don't have to be a master of all competencies, but these three are not negotiable.

Yes—they are that important.

Seven secrets gained over 37 years of navigating a career. Why is this book so very valuable for anyone who plans to earn a living? These pages reflect a unique journey; one I was very fortunate to navigate. Maybe somewhere out there is someone who survived more mergers, restructures, and downsizings than me. But frankly, I haven't met them yet.

This is how I did it.

PART ONE
THE COMPASS

THE COMPASS

"The pessimist complains about the wind; the optimist expects it to change; the realist adjusts the sail."

~William Arthur Ward

The inventions that have significantly shaped the course of mankind range from the atlatl (an ancient spear thrower) to the wheel to paper to the printing press to gunpowder to the automobile to the PC. Each innovation drastically advanced our development as a people, allowing man to progress from nomadic hunters to the architects of remarkable civilizations.

A part of that journey was made possible by the creation of the compass sometime around 1000 AD. It helped seafarers on voyages dependent on sighting land or following the stars reach a new world where direction could be plotted and planned—finally a device that transcended the storms.

Not so when it comes to most and their professional lives. No one shoves a GPS or a map into your hand and says, *"Follow this."* You use your instincts, you stumble, and in time—if you're lucky—you find that trail we talked about in the introduction.

Unfortunately, many only search. The facts back me up:

> • A 2013 Harris Poll suggested more than half of American workers wanted to change jobs.

- A stunning 80 percent of people in their 20s wanted to leave their current roles.

- With experience there was no guarantee of job satisfaction. Sixty-four percent of those in their 30s wanted to change or leave. That figure dropped to 54 percent by the time workers reached their 50s.

- A staggering 73 percent of all workers ended up in careers they hadn't planned on.

- A more recent Gallup Poll reinforced these finding with over half of workers indicating they were not engaged in their profession. Some of the greatest sufferers—the group the *New York Daily News* describes as the *"disenchanted millennials."*

One hundred thousand hours—and yet most, at best, endure. The chances are great that you will follow the suffering masses.

Surviving, especially in the corporate world, has never been more difficult. The days of career-long partnerships with corporations died in the '90s, replaced with nomadic arrangements that guarantee many who enter the business world will job hop throughout the course of their professional lives. The journey is made more arduous by the fact that many who embark on it do so with a level of naïveté that sometimes borders on the absurd. I include myself in this category. So little of what I assumed business and industry would be turned out to be accurate. For most there is no easy way to gain a sense of where you are—or where you're going. I know—I spent the first decade of my career trying to carve a path. Sometimes it was misguided. Sometimes it was the wrong direction. Sometimes I couldn't be sure if I should abandon my course or simply trudge on. To varying degrees that's true for most of us. And it's made more difficult by the fact that nothing in the corporate world—or in your company—will remain the same. There is constant transformation to match the demands of the market in which we compete. If you're not careful, you will find yourself crunched between the massive gears that must keep that machine rolling forward.

My own career evolved from the early days of trial-and-error. I marched through multiple jobs during my first 10 years—each with increasing levels of responsibility. I thought my career was soaring. I got paid a little bit more each time. My titles seemed (at least to me) more impressive. And then the day came that the company shifted and new leaders assumed responsibility—my path to the top suddenly less sure.

"What was this?" I thought to myself. *"Who changed the rules?"* I dug in, worked a little harder, re-established my credentials. And then it happened again. So I worked a little harder.

"I'll prove myself."

It was only after so many changes unfolded that it dawned on me one day that my course was terribly flawed. I would never be able to plot my path on the unpredictability of a supervisor, the company, or my industry. It was like trying to set my sail on a passing airplane in the night.

I needed a constant. And much to my chagrin, that constant was not going to be company issued.

My version of a career compass was born only when I began to look at my journey in a far different way.

The cardinal points began with establishing True North. Remember that the value of a compass as a navigational device is remarkably simple. It will always tell you where you are because its needle will always point north. Always. That constant allows the mariner to set his sail accordingly. It can be counted on.

There's an equal certainty in the corporate world.

PERSONAL ACCOUNTABILITY

It begins with you.

A million variables are at play when you start the climb we described in the introduction of the book. But early on you must reconcile that it's not just your chief or the instincts of your fellow hikers that will dictate how far you travel or the quality of that trek. The mountain will change. Your comrades will too. That chief you so depended on will likely not be with you long.

You are the constant. It is your performance, your goals, and your vision for your life that will dictate your future. For the remainder of your career it will be the one thing you can count on and that you can set your course around. Nothing else and no one else.

You will either fully invest in yourself or you will default to other directional points that you hope will guide you. And every one of them will fail.

Embrace the power of Personal Accountability. If you have established True North then the other cardinal points quickly become opportunities you will learn to navigate. Ignore Personal Accountability, and People, Process, and Perspective will be forever out of sync. Without the lodestar you will be left to wander.

THE OTHER POINTS ON THE COMPASS

People

Business is ultimately dependent on the success of people—not technology, brands, or strategy. That doesn't diminish the importance of each; it simply puts into perspective the fact that you are a part of an ecosystem that demands you can work with others. The reality is most of us either need to come equipped with or plan on developing uncommon people skills if we want to maximize our career journey.

Embedded here is the sometimes all-consuming influence of politics. If you're like most wandering into the corporate world, prepare to learn a lot about what and how people really work together—and how the factors behind the scene sometimes trump common sense.

Process

Every company has a way of working; systems that make the machine run. Included in these systems are highly refined processes that ensure the business is successful. And you can assume that understanding just how the whole works will take time and effort.

Acknowledge that one of the likely reactions you will have from time to time will be aggravation—and occasionally despair. Like our government, few companies operate at absolute effectiveness. Bureaucracy is certainly a part of the corporate world, and with virtually every career endeavor—as with politics—it was there before you arrived and will be there after you leave.

Perspective

"Everything we hear is an opinion, not a fact. Everything we see is a perspective, not the truth." ~**Marcus Aurelius**

There are probably more powerful and enduring aptitudes than perspective but I'm not sure if any are more important than this cardinal point as we try to establish equilibrium in our careers. I began mine believing the corporate world was a meritocracy and that most decisions were always just and fair—a naïve opinion. I was equally myopic as regards my own view of self.

The years taught me much. Your ability to build a truly balanced perspective—and to accept those things you can't change—is critical to your career survival.

STRAIGHT TALK

Think of it this way. There will always be just you, the people around you, the world that surrounds you, and how you interpret each. In the context of the opening of this book there will always be:

- You – the hiker (Personal Accountability)
- Your fellow hikers (People)
- The mountain and its nuances – weather, topography, etc. (Process)
- How you choose to look at the above three points (Perspective)

Sounds simple, doesn't it?

It's not. If it were, then a great many more would enjoy career success.

The Compass and its cardinal points represent four basic dimensions that most never think about and even fewer ever leverage. If you understand and apply its principles, you will navigate that trail we talked about—and ultimately forge your place.

Each of the chapters that follow is built around the 4 Ps of the Compass—and what they can really mean to your career.

PERSONAL ACCOUNTABILITY
T R U E   N O R T H

"You have brains in your head. You have feet in your shoes. You can steer yourself any direction you choose. You're on your own. And you know what you know. And YOU are the guy who'll decide where to go." ~Dr. Seuss

Get used to this simple fact: You'll start and end your corporate journey alone. Oh, there will be literally hundreds that will influence you along the way, but the footsteps you leave behind are just yours. That path you carve will reflect more than just your performance. It will speak to the balance you sought in your life, how well you conditioned yourself for the journey, and what degree of ownership you assumed in navigating your career.

I began my corporate life focused on the company and what I believed it demanded of me. Over the years I learned it was what I demanded of me that was far more important. The company would change, and the turnstile of departments I was a part of and bosses I reported to was never-ending.

I was the constant. And if I was going to survive I had to reconcile that one fact.

I became my own True North.

BRAND YOU

"When I was five years old my mother always told me
that happiness was the key to life. When I went to school
they asked me what I wanted to be when I grew up.
I wrote down 'happy.' They told me I didn't understand
the assignment and I told them they didn't understand life."

~John Lennon

Your first steps in your career can take years to complete. For most, the direction is murky at best. In my case, I was enamored with the notion of a big bonus and a company car, and the first legitimate offer I received I accepted.

I thought my life was complete. And then I walked into my first department meeting and realized every other person in the room was prepared to compete with me for compensation, recognition, and promotion.

And so one of my first corporate lessons began to take hold. It is a universal tenet.

Whether you go into operations, finance, technology, marketing, sales, advertising, or investment, you are now your own brand—not the role you play or the product you represent or the department you work in.

You.

If you're like most of us, your personal career plan is pretty primitive. Had you asked me about my goals in my first two years with the company my answer would have been remarkably simple—and equally naïve.

To do a good job and maybe get promoted.

Not exactly the stuff of legend. And then one day I found myself in a conversation with a peer talking about—of all things—sports. This was a colleague who seemed to invest every waking moment studying college football. He could give you point spreads, starting lineups, and virtually any statistic known to man. He loved the game. In fact, he couldn't shut up when the discussion turned to his favorite topic.

Not so for his professional life. The job, he said, didn't interest him much. It was just to pay the bills—nothing more. Until the day came that the company decided his services were no longer needed. My guess was he found another firm to fund his seats on the 50-yard line. But in his own way, he taught me something I've carried with me. It was his passion that drove him in one area, and his apathy that killed him in another.

Translation: This new world was likely going to change on me—a lot. If I were going to survive I needed motivators beyond title and paycheck (or the company car).

I had to find something I was actually passionate about.

That demanded I start to inventory my skills. I had to begin to ask myself what I actually enjoyed doing. It challenged me to forget what I was being paid and instead start to remember what I loved. That self-assessment helped me make decisions beyond survival—it helped me find meaning and purpose because it challenged me to grow.

And as I did an amazing thing happened.

I quit working in the conventional sense and much of my corporate environment became something of my own personal playground. That changed everything. My vision suddenly became clearer, my path infinitely simpler, and the beginnings of my personal brand took shape.

But finding that spark wasn't easy. It took me three different positions with the company before I stumbled into my passion. The reason: I never took the time to actually contemplate what I liked to do or wanted to do. Like most of my peers, I simply worked hard, hoped to distinguish myself, and prayed for good things to happen. I've just described a great many in the corporate world—each day they start out with a steady pace and a diligent stride, to nowhere.

Recognize this: Too many invest more time in considering their weekend social calendar or their choice of craft beers than in actually trying to find what excites them or where their real aptitudes lie. And even fewer in carving out a well-conceived career plan. Like my former colleague, their formula is remarkably naïve. Life is outside work—work is just… well, work. Their professional approach could be interpreted like this: no passion, no vision, no plan, no hope.

Many operate like a miner who walks into the middle of a local parking lot and proclaims to all that he will dig until he finds gold. Then he puts his head down and grimly goes to work, hoping and praying that someday he will strike it rich.

I mean, it could happen, right?

But then we could also base the essence of our financial plan on the assumption a meteor will someday hit us in the head and activate a portion of the brain that creates genius, resulting in our winning countless millions on a national game show.

Anything could happen. Our challenge is to influence the odds in our favor to best impact what we want to happen. And a passion-driven vision combined with focused planning can be a game changer.

So let's call out the first major pitfall for a majority of people—it's easier not to plan. Planning requires vision. It requires thought. It demands we look beyond the end of our nose and actually attempt to describe our ideal future. Most prefer to take things as they happen or *"shoot from the hip."*

Get used to it—you are the most important brand you will ever represent. No one else will help you promote yourself more than you will help you promote yourself. Don't assume there are benevolent overlords in the corridors of power who are constantly trolling to help the next generation succeed. Oh, there are people who will care, who will help—but the sooner you divorce yourself from old paradigms the better equipped you will be to navigate your own career path.

I've spent a lot of years talking to employees who had ambitious goals for their life, but stunningly few who had actually found a driving force that could propel them. Every goal is only a dream unless there's a passion that fuels it. And all the wishes in the world are meaningless unless there's a well-conceived plan to realize them.

Unfortunately, a great many never get there. They settle on a job. They give up on a meaningful career.

STRAIGHT TALK

Make the decision to find something you're passionate about, and assume it may take a few job changes to get there. Yes, there will be some effort involved but simply settling for a paycheck will likely ensure your brand will falter. If you have no idea of where your strengths or aptitudes really are, then find out—and soon. Invest in a book like StrengthsFinders 2.0 by Tom Rath. It's a fantastic resource to do your personal inventory. More important, it can offer you a vehicle to think in larger terms than just the present.

Remember, the constant for your compass begins with Personal Accountability. Personal Accountability begins with a high degree of self-awareness. Your brand doesn't start with a clear strategy until you've taken the time to examine where your skills and your interests lie. The brand will never flourish if you haven't found a place and a role that excites you. You can't market apathy and you can't market mediocrity.

OWNING VS RENTING

*"It takes courage to grow up and become
who you really are."*

~E. E. Cummings

"So, what do you want to be when you grow up?"

Remember that question your Aunt Edna used to ask at the holiday dinners? And you would stammer out some inane response about the things that captured your imagination. Fireman, astronaut, nurse, Olympic speed skater, president, or tank commander—whatever it was, it came from the heart and it didn't have to make a lot of sense. And Aunt Edna would smile and reassure you that it would come to be, and you promptly went back to your turkey leg. Those questions subsided in time. You went to school. You got a job. Your professional life got underway.

And chances are good you no longer asked yourself what you wanted to be—you just became.

But Aunt Edna served an important purpose beyond bringing the macaroni casserole. At some level she made you at least consider a question that stymies many of us as we grow into adulthood.

"What do I want to be?"

If you want to survive it's a question you will ask yourself a lot—and over the course of your career. But maintaining that inner voice can be difficult. It can be silenced by the mind-numbing cadence of meetings, deadlines, and reports. Oh, it's there. We just have to find a way to tap into it.

The challenge is to ask ourselves the right questions—the ones that force us to really think about our goals in life, not simply act; the ones that force us to move beyond the comfort level of the status quo and to truly grow. Many (especially in the corporate world) devote their time to title and compensation; far less on what their aptitudes are and where their true passions lay.

And they resign themselves to working a job for the rest of their lives—never tapping into their real potential.

I have met very few true champions in the corporate world who don't enjoy asking themselves tough questions.

You will have only one life coach over the course of your career. Oh, there will be a great many external mentors, guides, teachers, and consultants, but the reality is there is only one who will stay with you for the entire ride.

You.

There is an opposite approach, and I've seen it a thousand times. Instead of asking ourselves the questions that challenge us, we allow others to do it for us. We call those people our supervisors, or managers, or directors, or corporate heads. And so we effectively abdicate accountability for our development to someone else.

I can still remember a conversation early in my career with a manager on the subject of my personal development. I was eager and ambitious. I wanted to know what I should do and what timelines I should plan around to realize my goals over the next few years. His response, *"You're too young to even consider that next step for at least five years."* I asked why—was it a function of my current performance or my lack of skills? His answer, *"That's just how we do things."* Here's what I learned. The *"how we do things"* meant he had no clue. So I decided how we do things was going to change.

The survivors I've met in industry are the ones who embraced full responsibility—every step—for their career. That doesn't mean you don't rely on others; no one makes it alone. But you can rent your career accountability or you can own your career accountability.

If you've ever had occasion to own a rental property, you have probably dealt with the challenges of property management. And you learn pretty quickly that not all renters are created equal. There are some who will treat your house like it was theirs and others who will treat it like the Motel 6 party hall.

You look for those who will behave like owners. Owners have more than a monthly payment to consider. They have a mortgage. And when you mortgage something you treat it differently.

The same holds true for your career plan. If you've decided to abdicate accountability or shift it to someone else—whether to your company or your boss—you have just become a renter. You've taken away your mortgage on your professional life and said, *"I will pay you with my time and my effort and in turn you will provide me with a safe place."*

Big mistake. At that point you have just sold your ownership stake in your future and made yourself subject to others pulling you along. You've just become an employee and not an entrepreneur.

Listen to that voice inside of you, the one that fuels your passion and longs to drive your career. Make your experiences and how you react to them your primary teacher, not the latest company sponsored resource or the next great manager known for developing others.

Become an owner.

STRAIGHT TALK

Aunt Edna had the right idea. The problem for most is they stop asking themselves that very question once they become adults. They settle into a job that pays the bills or offers security. Life takes over and those heady dreams of youth give way to reality. But what if you could go back and answer that question again not saddled with the mortgage or the car payments? The question changes now; instead of what do you want to be it becomes what can you be?

A DIFFERENT DRUMMER

"The person who follows the crowd will usually go no further than the crowd. The person who walks alone is likely to find himself in places no one has ever seen before."

~Albert Einstein

On any given Sunday if you choose to frequent your local mall you will likely notice the occasional gaggle of young teenagers that rove the food court and the retail stores—a tight cluster of 14- and 15-year-olds who seem to move as one.

My wife always points to the adolescent girls and comments on how they dress the same, talk the same, hold their hands the same way, and chatter nervously as they attempt to move through a world they are not yet comfortable in navigating.

Even a jaded observer would note the one thing every one of them wants to avoid is in anyway looking different. Peer pressure to conform is probably about the highest it will ever be.

But the notion of the *"herd mentality"* is not limited to your local mall or the plains of the Serengeti. It plays a role in your career too—even when we grow gray. It becomes easier and easier to look like everyone else, talk like everyone else, and yes, think like everyone else. Many consider it a critical survivor skill.

I'm not so sure.

None of us has an infinite amount of time and energy to power our career, and yet far too many default to conformity.

Work hard, say the right things, keep your head down, and wait for the skies to clear. I call this the *"Wish Upon a Star Plan."* The logic being: I'm better off keeping my mouth shut and doing my job than in creating ripples. Maybe my company doesn't want innovation or strategic thinking. It just wants me to do what I'm paid to do.

Rich Horwath's book *Deep Dive* contains a fascinating idea he calls the Principle of Competitive Exclusion. It's based on the assumption that when like species engaged in the very same activities are forced to coexist, both will not survive.

Translation: If you behave just like everybody else (perform the same activities), you must either do those activities differently to distinguish yourself or you must choose to perform different activities.

Two classic examples are the Mini Cooper and legendary country singer Johnny Cash. Horwath suggests that each became uniquely successful because they were—well—uniquely unique. Cash came along at a time when his baritone voice and everyman appeal struck a chord very different from the mainstream. He was not polished and he was not packaged. And audiences fell in love with him—from the black outfits he evolved into wearing as his popularity grew to his opening line to his fans.

"Hello...I'm Johnny Cash."

It was like the old boy on the barstool beside you had just decided to walk up onstage and give singing a whirl.

The Mini Cooper was underpowered, looked a little like a souped-up golf cart, and abruptly blew the doors off of the competition.

Why? Some might say it was because they chose a truly different path to build competitive advantage.

I think we see examples of that every day. Remember the rise of Madonna or Lady Gaga, the bombastic appeal of sports promoter Don King, or the overwhelming appeal of the survivor reality shows a few years back? The 2016 national political elections reinforced the *"power of different"* even more. In each of these cases the public responded to individuals who effectively broke the mold.

I've thought often about the Principle of Competitive Exclusion and its application to corporate survival.

There is a push to the middle that challenges us for much of our career, and certainly in the business world. Just like those teenage girls at the mall, few want to stand too far outside the mainstream. There's safety in sameness. And yet you have to ask yourself how much have you distinguished yourself from the norm, if at all?

When I think back to the countless thousands of employees I've met over the course of my career I find myself remembering most the few who were, in their own way, truly different. They found a way to parlay their unique talents and resources in such a way that it allowed them to stand out from the norm.

Does that mean we each don a silver tuxedo and show up at the next meeting strumming a ukulele? No, but sometimes the courage to step outside the boundaries of the conventional can be incredibly powerful.

The corporate world doesn't make it easy but then again if it were easy anybody could do it. There is no absolute standard in your career that demands you talk and think like everyone else.

Remember, your role in the company and in your job is going to be defined—but only to a point. One of your challenges will be to decide how you expand your position, develop new ideas, and build on the obvious expectations. You operate in what is essentially a learning laboratory. Systems, processes, strategies, structure, and brands all conspire to create more than their share of challenges. Problems abound. The individuals who demonstrate the creativity to find solutions can reshape their world and recreate their jobs. I've seen numerous examples of employees who basically wrote a new job description because of extra assignments they took on to enhance their value to the organization.

So much of your personal branding is dependent on your ability to differentiate yourself—unique sells.

STRAIGHT TALK

The corporate world homogenizes—so do most careers. You will not survive if you commit to always just following the crowd.

BURNOUT & BALANCE
Work Better, Not Harder

"You can do anything but not everything."
~David Allen

No matter what you may be told, your career is a series of sprints and not a marathon. Tony Schwartz's book *The Way We're Working Isn't Working* speaks to a phenomenon I truly did not appreciate for the first half of my career. The message—long, hard hours of effort do not necessarily equate to success. Our bodies, our minds, and our spirits require periods of rest and renewal. Peak performance requires corresponding periods of peak rest. It allows you to fully recover and helps make certain you are *"on your game"* when you need to be.

Work-life balance is more than a Human Resources-generated catchphrase. In my world, I never saw a grinder win the game of Corporate Survivor. Some made it to the finish line but they never realized their full potential.

One of the real extreme danger zones in your career journey is burnout. There are a number of definitions around this phenomenon, but basically it can best be described as that jumping-off point when an individual has so worked himself or herself to a point of mental exhaustion that they can't go further. And it is an affliction you will see often in the world of business. Many of the most effected victims suffer an even more ominous fate—they're either left to suffer an "on the job" death where they can't afford to leave but don't know how to take the steps to find a healthier work environment, or the company makes the decision for them. Either can effectively end your career. The first scenario is a form of corporate purgatory. The latter can be hell.

I remember when I finally came to grips with the fact that competitive people gravitate to the corporate world for a reason; it's the best place in the world to test your skills and abilities against others. And success there is just like salt water to a dying man—the more you drink, the thirstier you get.

The toughest thing for many high achievers is taking the time to rest, to recuperate, and to recharge. I know—I had the same challenge in my career. Fortunately, many of the 20-somethings entering the corporate world today have a more realistic perspective on business than some of the preceding generations. They've witnessed firsthand the pitfalls of industry, and in many cases, have dealt with fathers and mothers negatively impacted by the idiosyncrasies of corporate life. That's created a more objective view of how important your job is in the overall scheme of things.

For all of us, the legacy we leave behind will likely be found in our families and in the impact we've had on others. The corporate carrot can be powerful, but it is only a carrot. The salary increases and titles gray with time. The real diamonds lay somewhere else. You will never find them if you allow your focus to become so blurred that you never take the time to look.

Very early on in your career you may find yourself struggling to strike a balance between your business and personal life.

Here are a few **Burnout Balancing Tips** for you to consider, regardless of your field of endeavor:

> • Don't fall into the *"activity for activity's sake"* trap that afflicts many companies and many individuals. Your colleague comes in at 7 a.m. so you make certain you're there at 6:30. Your office mate works late every evening so you do the same. Even more egregious—trying to impress your boss by outworking him, or always being *"on call."* Too many confuse activity with accomplishment. Don't be one of them.

> • The same holds true for the phenomenon I call Cell Hell, best described as the black hole of late night or early morning cell phone give-and-take that

some decide is their sole ticket to productivity. I once had a manager who I was convinced waited for Sunday afternoon to start making calls. The real message, "My work is my life." He succeeded only in angering his "followership" and convincing many he would be better served in becoming a taxi dispatcher.

• Decide what's really most important in your life and make certain to align your activities to those guiding principles. I've worked with scores of people who trumpet their focus on family and then promptly spend most of their time at the office or on the job—including giving back vacation. Trust me when I say when you approach retirement no one will step forward to give you that time back.

Burnout is a self-inflicted wound. Your choice if you decide to pull the trigger.

STRAIGHT TALK

Hard work must be followed by hard rest. Forget the activity traps. Like an oasis in the hot desert they obscure the reality of survival.

Fall for them and you're only fooling yourself.

B U R N O U T & B A L A N C E
Part 2: Going Pro

"Commitment is an act, not a word."

- **Jean-Paul Sartre**

I liken much of the corporate world to the playing field of professional sports: intense, competitive, and yes, a game. But unlike your favorite athlete, there is no TV crew examining your every move or dissecting your performance.

There is only you, the boss who supervises you, and the company that chooses to offer you a paycheck.

So now you get compensated to go out and provide a work product. The company, in effect, rents your behavior and in turn expects your commitment to deliver.

You've *"gone pro"* as a Corporate Athlete.

Now you will either make the team or you will be cut. And if you're playing Varsity expect a lot of cuts.

Like any great athlete you will win only if you are well prepared, well trained, and conditioned to succeed. You may not be walking onto a playing field in a traditional sense, but it is a playing field nonetheless. Your ability to compete will be dependent on how well you maintain your conditioning—physically, emotionally, spiritually, and mentally—over the course of your career.

Show me a true corporate champion and I will show you someone who recognized long ago that balance in his or her life was the only way to sustain success. Vice versa, the list of *"players"* who burned out—suffered physical problems, emotional meltdowns, and spiritual crisis—was endless.

So here then is one of the answers I've offered to many over the years when they ask my secret to surviving the roller coaster. I call the suggestions below **The Burnout Busters** because every one of them helped me sustain a course when I saw others fall by the wayside. If you believe that your North Star is Personal Accountability, then commit to each—and soon:

- Find a gym. Join it. And then actually use it. Routinely. Your body can pay a toll in the corporate world, if you allow it to happen. Train like an athlete—perform like an athlete. Train like a spectator—expect to eventually have a nice seat in the bleachers.

- Make a commitment to understanding diet, and make healthy eating a part of your daily habits. Travel and the associated nuances can play havoc with what you eat and when you eat. You'll either learn to negotiate that or you will develop problems. I've watched too many colleagues battle health problems because of an inability to learn basic nutritional guidelines.

- Embrace your friends. Social outlets are critical. And if your only outlet is your job—you are holding on far too tight. The job is fickle. It will love you at times and it will hate you at times, but it will always look at you through green-tinted glasses—yes, the same color as the dollars that power it.

- Find a life partner who "gets it" and can support you. If you're lucky you'll find someone who helps you put things into perspective and not be sucked into the tornado. I married "up." My wife has always manned the fort that is the Cole household. She has made my career infinitely easier as a result.

- If you choose to drink alcohol, limit it and do not make it a part of your work life—including off-site business meetings. I've seen multiple careers interrupted because of booze and drugs. And a general rule I have espoused for three decades—nothing good happens after midnight at company functions.

• Recognize and embrace your faith. There will be numerous opportunities where you will recognize the failures of man (and the corporate world). All of them can be placed in better context when balanced against a higher order. The former will never be perfect. I believe the latter always will be.

• Develop and nourish hobbies outside of work. Far too many make their vocation their avocation—a terrible mistake. A simple guideline for you, if by the fourth day of vacation you're anxious about work, your interests may be far too narrow. There is life outside of your career but you need to build it. Our home is filled with evidence of hobbies I've cultivated over the years—and continue to build.

• Stay active. Amazing how many people I've watched grow old because of a sedentary lifestyle. Those habits compromise you in your 30s and 40s. They can kill you in your 50s and 60s.

• Continue to stimulate your most important muscle, your mind. It can be and should be a passion that sustains you long after your career is done. As I write these words I am reminded that my lifelong interest in better understanding personal leadership continues to be a companion that travels with me. Its study inspires and sustains me, and has helped me to look at a large part of the world around me as something of a learning laboratory. The body will grow old. I pray my mind will stay forever young.

One of the best books on the subject of balancing your life is *The Corporate Athlete Advantage* by Jim Loehr and Jack Groppel. I am a devotee of their principles and the practical advice they offer in harnessing energy for the long career haul.

Your career is going to knock you down from time to time. No matter—the well-conditioned athlete finds a way to get back up. But only if you treat your body as any player would.

If you're lucky, it will last you a lifetime.

STRAIGHT TALK

There are four dimensions to your health and well-being. They extend far beyond your professional life. The physical, emotional, social, and spiritual aspects of your world are like table legs. If one collapses then the whole follows. Take the steps to nourish each and your chances for survival increase. Ignore one and you will ultimately pay the price.

FREE AGENCY

"The only thing I know for sure
is that I know nothing at all, for sure."

~Socrates

Congratulations, you have the job you've always dreamed of. Hopefully it is a position that ensures you are enhancing your skill set and truly beginning to optimize your full potential.

Now, just when you are blinded by the brilliance of your genius, do yourself one more favor.

Get the résumé out—the one that landed you this plumb position. Put it in your top drawer and Time Activate your planner to review and modify that résumé at least once per quarter—every quarter—for the rest of your career.

Even if that means a brief review and a few edits to reflect modifications or new skills or experiences.

Whether this is your first job or your 10th, chances are good (especially in the corporate world) you will need to pull it out again.

Your skills are the engine that will keep your career on the road.

But if you're like most people, you'll move immediately to put that glossy brochure that showcases the engine up on a shelf. And wait until necessity demands you find it, dust it off, and try to make sense of it again.

A recipe for disaster.

You never stop looking at opportunities. You never shut yourself off from networking and building your sphere of influence.

And you never let your résumé just gather dust. It's like your personal version of a jet fighter—ready to go at a moment's notice.

Keep an Accomplishments log, even if it is a very general summation of what you do. The content may not make its way to your résumé but it will inform your Performance Reviews and it will add gravitas to your discussions with your current manager or the new company you're talking to.

Remember, your future employment is always dependent on producing results today, not how hard you work or how well-intentioned you might be. I've had hundreds of applicants profess their commitment to excellence. I only hire or promote those who can show me their commitment to excellence.

Most sports fans are very familiar with the term *"free agent."* In the athletic world it means the player is not under any binding contract and is free to sign with any team willing to enter into an arrangement deemed acceptable to both parties.

Free agents sometimes can command astonishing salaries and can tip the balance sheet immeasurably when they "hit the market."

Here's one of the *"ahas"* I want to impress on the reader that may run contrary to established convention, but whether you want to accept it or not, is very real in the corporate world and for most careers.

From the day you walk onto your first playing field to the day you walk away—you are a Free Agent.

Unless you are one of the fortunate few who signs an employment contract (and how binding those are is debatable), you and virtually everyone in your company is just like that NFL cornerback who is on the open market.

There is no corporate obligation to pick up your *"contract,"* and without it they can let you walk at any given time and for a myriad of reasons. If you want to believe you are forever tied to your organization because you're a producer, a top performer, or an all-around nice guy then you probably should sign agreements to work with the Tooth Fairy and the Easter Bunny.

They're both about as lucrative when it comes to wish lists.

Many newcomers have a hard time embracing the fact that organizational reshuffles can eliminate their job immediately. Understandable—no one wants to believe their next paycheck could be their last.

But it could be, and sometimes is.

I've seen far too many enormously talented individuals watch their roles vanish and then react with shock that rivals victims of a street mugging.

"How could they have done this to me?"

It's business folks. Get over it.

Free agency is real. Your willingness to accept and confront that reality is part of your maturation as a Career Survivor.

So, if you buy even part of this supposition, what do you do about it?

For your consideration, the all-important **Free Agent Four**:

- From the first hour of your first day, begin to build your skills based on the assumption that your job will someday end. Make certain you are building a résumé that will ensure that even if it does, your career will continue. The goal of this book isn't to make certain you invest your professional life with one company— it's to make sure you build a sustainable career.

- Craft a verifiable record of production. Performance rules in the corporate world. That résumé we mentioned at the beginning of this chapter—at best it will only open a door to other opportunities outside the company. Interviewers will look at two things when they talk to you—what you've done and what you say. Of the two, performance is the one that will be focused on by the best firms. I wish I could remember every candidate who told me in an interview they were a rock star but couldn't produce a track record that proved it. No proof—it didn't happen.

- Expand beyond the traditional. The top companies— especially in a down market—will have their choice of qualified candidates. Delivering the basics of your current role guarantees you very little in a *"buyers' choice"* environment. Take on growth opportunities, lead task forces, and demonstrate personal leadership. Average is for the competitors—the best want only the best.

- Network beyond the boundaries of your company—one of the least understood but one of the most important skills for any person walking the corporate trail. If you can join industry committees, do it. If you can connect with others in the business, take every advantage. If you can build quality relationships with persons higher in your company or others, optimize them. If you can fully leverage the power of social media, do it. And incidentally, recognize what networking is not—reaching out to that senior contact when your job has ended and you're looking for work. Seen this more times than I can recount. That's not networking, that's manipulating relationships for personal gain—and it seldom pays off.

There's no one in the corporate world that doesn't yearn for job security, but your only security is housed in the unique skills you build. The days of lifetime arrangements have passed. As the primary architect, you own every aspect of your career. Every employee—whether they're at six months, six years, or 26 years—needs to consider whether they have an exit strategy. The core of that strategy will always be transferrable skills.

Companies pay only for proven talent. Your time with a given organization could end tomorrow. Hopefully, your career will not.

STRAIGHT TALK

If you knew for certain your last paycheck would be delivered in six months, would you do something different today? If the answer is yes then give some hard thought to how you much you have embraced the Free Agent principles outlined above. The average job lasts just over four years. Do the math.

WALKING AWAY

"Don't be afraid to give up the good, to go for the great."
~John D. Rockefeller

You play this game of corporate long enough and you will inevitably find yourself in situations you consider untenable.

Dead-end position. Dying division. Pending organizational downsizing. Role about to be eliminated. Boss who is driving you nuts. Department filled with malcontents.

The list is potentially endless.

A great many achievers populate your world and one of the toughest challenges many of them face is in deciding when or if it's time to walk away.

Quitting is not a part of many people's DNA. It wasn't part of mine either.

But one of the beauties of our free-enterprise system is the fact that none of us are committed to a life of indentured servitude. There are no manacles that force us to restrict our lives to one company or one department.

Your bonds with your company are not unlike a marriage. Check that—an *"involved"* relationship.

And as with every relationship, sometimes you must make decisions that are difficult.

Over the course of 30-plus years, I've faced that choice on several occasions. And I've watched trusted friends and colleagues struggle with it as well.

Some went on to make well-informed choices while others—well, they just reacted.

A separation in the business world can be initiated by either party. I call the questions below the **Corporate Divorce Ten**. Whether you're well into your career or just starting out, it will behoove you to consider them if and when you reach your own crossroad. Your answers should dictate whether you file the papers for separation or stay with the company you've chosen. They are:

- Am I truly happy here?
- Are this company's values and philosophies aligned with mine?
- Am I passionate about what I do every day?
- Do my skill sets align with what I do?
- Is my role rewarding, and does it offer me a future?
- What are my options internally and have I explored them?
- Have I consulted with my mentors?
- What happens if I do nothing at all?
- What are my options outside the company?
- What happens if I leave?

Sometimes there is honor in walking away, especially when you are drowning.

STRAIGHT TALK

Job terminations are a two-way street. It's not always the company that's forced to fire. Sometimes in the corporate world you must make one of the most difficult of decisions: to have the courage to let the company go—to terminate your relationship because of its failure to perform.

When that happens, thank them for their service.

Wish them well.

Move on.

PEOPLE

"Before you criticize someone, walk a mile in their shoes. That way, you'll be a mile from them, and you'll have their shoes."
~ Jack Handey

One of the most influential mentors in my career constantly reminded me of a timeless principle in business. *"Tim,"* he said, *"Never forget our most valuable resource drives home every day. You figure out how to invest in people and all the other stuff will get a lot, lot easier."*

I watched him place that simple approach at the top of everything he did, and I learned the value of my company and the success of my personal journey would always be measured by an intangible that wasn't easy to capture on an income statement. In the years that followed, I learned a lot more about assets, cash, profit, and growth, but the simplicity of that early tenet never left me.

People are the second cardinal point of the Compass. Those that survive in their corporate journey begin to appreciate early on that it involves a lot more than knowing the names on the company roster or who works beside you in the next cubicle. Whether you're a newcomer or a veteran, it's your ability to work with everyone—not just those you like or who share similar views—that will ultimately distinguish you.

And trust me when I say that negotiating the unpredictable nature of human relations challenges all. The cast of characters that will dance across your career stage will never cease to surprise you.

The heartbeat of your company comes from the people who walk in the door every day. They create the culture and they can flame the passion—or they can destroy the greatest strategy in the world. They are the lifeblood and the most important asset on any balance sheet.

If you believe that intellect and innate skills will sustain you without advanced people acumen—good luck. Maybe you're lucky enough to make it on just your own drive. I haven't met one who did. Misanthropes are left behind.

What follows are practical lessons in the all-important arena of People.

WE'RE ALL ONE BIG, HAPPY FAMILY ...

"The only people I owe my loyalty to are those who never made me question theirs."

~Anonymous

At the beginning of the book I talked about what I wish someone would have told me when I embarked on my journey. Here's one of the essentials. I've made it the first chapter under People for a reason. One of the lessons of a corporate veteran—you can and should respect and honor the company that employs you, but your loyalties should be reserved for individuals, not corporations.

Corporations are driven by profit and can, often do, change personalities at the whim of a board or an incoming president or CEO. There are massive factors that influence large companies and one thing is certain—their memory is only as long as the latest earnings report.

Today's generation of newcomers understands that fact well. My generation — well, we had to learn the hard way. Many of us went to work believing hard work and commitment guaranteed us the corporate equivalent of the *"tenure"* granted in the academic world. Culture and vision statements spoke of family and many of the value propositions could have been clipped from a Boy Scout's manual.

But the rise of a true global economy and diminishing margins changed that dynamic in the '90s. In the health-care industry big companies began to swallow smaller ones, and even bigger companies were merging with like-sized competitors. It became a fight for survival as pipelines began to shrink and blockbuster new brands dwindled.

Meanwhile, my little company had grown exponentially—becoming a lucrative investment stock—just as whispers of restructurings and downsizings began to filter their way into the hallway chatter.

But many of us still labored under an already dead paradigm—work hard and your career was safe.

Until it wasn't.

And so began the first of the great downsizing tsunamis. New corporate terms emerged, and catchphrases with words like *"re-engineering, right-sizing, headcount adjustments, structural optimization, and role elimination"* became a part of industry parlance.

The old agreements were ripped away. Almost overnight the assumption that a company choice might be a lifetime decision went with it. It was a brutal awakening that extended far beyond my firm's boundaries—a cold splash of reality I would never forget.

Lesson learned—no company is a family. The corporate world is not a place where like- minded individuals gather to spend their professional lives living happily ever after.

It's a universe forged by a collection of people accountable for driving profitability for whoever writes their paycheck. Philanthropy, beneficence, and loyalty may be a part of your company's culture, but when profit margins narrow or when earnings reports teeter, the greatest capital cost will likely be the first trimmed.

Which is why I learned to reserve my true loyalties for people.

And the list—if I were to be completely honest—has always been incredibly short. Some of them I worked for, some I worked alongside, and some worked for me. But make no mistake, it was my loyalty to people that helped me survive.

STRAIGHT TALK

Find a half dozen people who you truly trust at any given time in your career and you are remarkably fortunate. Hopefully, they are credible, competent, and have your best interests at heart.

Loyalty—it belongs with people and people only.

REMEMBER YOUR
WAITERS AND WAITRESSES

"How they treat you defines them.
How you treat others defines you."

~Rita Zahara

One of the first real-life laboratories I was able to experience in my formative years was when I was invited to join a senior colleague at an upscale restaurant. Fine dining, complete with a wine steward and a level of service that surpassed any I had experienced. The food was great and the ambiance impressive. It should have been quite an evening—except for my colleague and how he chose to deal with the *"hired help."*

Condescending, dismissive, and little to no patience. He berated our server, returned three bottles of wine because they didn't suit his taste, and generally made an ass of himself. Then he turned back to me and turned on the charm—as if the person he was just talking to was invisible.

I was shocked. I had no real gravitas with the company and certainly didn't command any particular level of respect. The one thing I did have was the beginnings of a career and some degree of a reputation for performance.

In other words, he needed me. And he needed me to like him; hence, my invitation to join his highness for this rare evening of high-priced fare. My guess is that he did more damage to our relationship than he could have in a year of working together.

And he had no idea.

In the years since, I've seen similar patterns of behavior from individuals who consider themselves people of power—on airplanes, in retail stores, at hotel check out desks, and in just about every walk of life.

And I've learned that one of the best indicators of the real merits of an individual can be gauged in how they interact with those they consider less than their equal, without influence; yes—subservient.

There is no aristocracy or proletariat in our country—at least in terms of how we should deal with others. But there is a class bias, and some of the worst offenders demonstrate their own inadequacies every day.

Character can be difficult to determine in the professional arena. Maybe it's because there are a lot of *"character actors"* out there who can and often do disguise themselves with a blanket of corporate manners that cloaks their personality. But watching how people interact with others away from the job can sometimes offer one heck of a window.

I believe some of the people I have admired most in my professional life must have decided at some point in their journey that basic human dignity was more than a corporate competency, it was a part of their personal value system. And I watched them treat everyone from division heads to the guy who vacuumed the hall in exactly the same way—with courtesy and respect.

STRAIGHT TALK

There's a lot of gamesmanship in any profession and certainly in corporate. The lights of center stage can be blinding. If you really want to understand the character of a colleague at any level, it's sometimes best to get them away from where they focus on the role they believe they're required to play.

Take them to lunch.

THE DANCE
OF THE TOADIES

"Leaders don't create followers, they create more leaders."

~Tom Peters

OK, let's keep it real here. If you have spent even three months in your business life or career you have seen the dance.

Everyone has.

It's the one that forms around the person in a position of authority that always kicks in at the social gatherings, the break rooms, and the meetings.

The cluster of underlings who flock around the Alpha to laugh at the jokes, to fawn at his or her comments, and to marvel at their genius.

Working it.

I call it The Dance of the Toadies. Said another way; the unctuous subservience some make their priority in trying to advance their career. No, let's call it what it really is—*"kissing up."*

To varying degrees, all of us are Toadies at some point in our professional journey. Very few can avoid it. It's human nature to instinctively defer to the leader of the tribe, and my guess is that it is mired in our DNA—a remnant of our distant past that cannot be completely exorcised.

But the corporate world has its own special melody.

Here all are scrambling to make a name and establish their place in the pecking order. What better way than to play up to the boss?

There are some who are masters. You'll watch them move on a beeline when the opportunity presents, sometimes hopping over other Toadies just as eager to make their presence known. And very few of us have not been there ourselves.

And let's keep it just as real when we say there are many organizations and frankly, many leaders, who turn up the speakers for the dance. This is their moment in the spotlight. How many other times in their life will they ever feel more important, more admired, or more powerful?

It can kill a company and it can also suck the lifeblood out of your career.

So how do you manage to either avoid the dance or at least put it into proper perspective? A few thoughts for you to consider—here then, **The Toadie Watch Outs**:

> • The Dance is a cultural ceremony that borders on offering up sacrifices to craven images; your purchase of everlasting life in the corporate heavens. Some will give up their personal integrity or even their values in sacrifice. Are people able to dance their way to career success? Sometimes. But when the music stops so does their career.

> • There is a risk in the Dance. Most leaders of even modest awareness know the song and they know the dancers. And even the neediest leaders see it for what it is, maybe because some of them were are are Toadies themselves.

> • The best leaders are the ones who will respond the least to the Dance. Many of them are more inclined to seek out others than to be the center of the circle. They'll recognize the empty plaudits for what they are, and will also note that your behavior around them is markedly different than with others.

> • At one time or another all of us are Toadies. Every time you choose not to speak openly, every time you amend your behavior to account for someone in a position of authority, every time you compromise your values in order to accommodate—you're guilty of Toadie behavior. There are those out there who have

made a career out of being a Toadie. They've sacrificed personal integrity to get a *"Pass Go"* to the next job.

I would submit that the sacrifice is too great.

The Dance of the Toadies is a part of most but not all corporate cultures, and it will be engrained into almost every career field. It is a learned step and how far out on the floor you choose to go is up to you. The people I have admired most in my professional life are those few who managed to hum along but never really picked up the beat. They were outstanding team players who were strong enough never to *"play the game."* I saw them as fiercely independent individuals who valued those around them, but would not subordinate their standards in order to appease someone else.

And for what it's worth, I've been at the center of that circle I talked about earlier quite a few times too. I've managed thousands of people and I'm certain I've encouraged Toadishness from time to time by my behaviors. But with each passing year I've grown more tired of the song.

STRAIGHT TALK

Toadies are part of the corporate world but they do not make great companies. Great companies want true contributors—individuals of high character who are able to think for themselves and not just "play the part"; leaders capable of questioning the status quo and providing legitimate input—not just compliance.

So, do Toadies have a place?

Absolutely.

Hollywood is always looking for studio audience members for game shows, late-night talk formats, and of course, infomercials.

E M U s

"Whenever you commend, add your reasons for doing so;
it is this which distinguishes the approbation
of a man of sense from the flattery of sycophants
and the admiration of fools."

~Sir Richard Steele

At some point in your professional career you will begin to get acquainted with a skill set seldom talked about but critical to your survival in the corporate world. It's an often misunderstood talent but one that all of us—to some degree—will demonstrate.

Managing up can be defined as follows: the capacity to effectively lead your leader, best demonstrated by the proactive job behaviors you exhibit on a daily basis, your willingness to only follow their lead, and the various social behaviors that suggest blind support for their position.

You won't find that definition in most books on management by the way, but it is very real and you will not pass through the corporate jungle without gaining an appreciation for it.

There are masters of the art out there, some who will rise very high in your organization because they made who they report to their primary focal point.

The acronym I use to identify these Experts at Managing Up—EMUs. With apologies to the Australian bird of the same name, I coined the term because it reminded me so much of the Road Runner from those old Looney Tune cartoons some of us grew up with. EMUs in the career arena can sometimes accelerate very quickly, leaving a lot of coyotes in the dust.

Managing up is not necessarily a bad thing. The challenge begins when the skill of navigating your relationship with your supervisor/leader/manager takes the place of true competency in your role.

And do not believe for a second that this does not happen—and often—in the corporate world and in most fields.

Every day.

In the course of my career I've witnessed periods where employees were compelled to devote more attention to their line leader than to their jobs. And that created the ideal petri dish to cultivate and grow EMUs.

Let me be clear—there is a very real difference between true followership and managing up. The first is a necessary component of every successful company, team, business unit or military regiment. Without followership, organizations of every type break down and chaos replaces order. No leader in history has achieved success without the willing capacity of others to follow. It is an immutable law.

But managing up can be and sometimes is the dirty underbelly of followership. Often it represents a conscious effort on behalf of the subordinate to manipulate for personal gain, not just for organizational effectiveness.

You will not spend more than a year in corporate without seeing artists at making the boss feel good. Many make their careers by becoming Super EMUs.

I learned a valuable lesson in how to put the skill set in proper perspective early in my career. I worked alongside a peer who could not rush quickly enough to agree with our supervisor on any issue—whether it involved company policy, a brand strategy, or completing an expense report. My guess was that if our manager expressed support for mass suicide my colleague would have stood and led the charge to purchase the cyanide pills. In fact, it became a game among others to time how long in any meeting before he offered enthusiastic support for whatever came out of the manager's mouth.

And yet an unusual phenomenon occurred after the formal meeting. No one was more critical of our direction than that very same peer.

Public affirmation—private criticism. My first exposure to an EMU.

But I watched it become a very slippery slope for my colleague. In his zeal to build a level of influence with his formal manager he was destroying the respect of his peers. He had made a conscious decision to tether his success to another; and in doing that he was losing ground in becoming a leader in the organization.

In the ensuing years I would watch multiple colleagues compromise their own integrity to *"win points."* But whatever tally sheet they were focusing on was actually robbing them.

To be sure, everyone, to some degree, manages up. The question you have to answer for yourself is simply this: *"Am I charged with making my boss the focus of my job, or am I charged with making the focus of my job—my job?"*

If you spend most of your professional time trying to anticipate your boss's needs, congratulations, you've made managing up your priority. You may enjoy a high degree of success but you will never realize your true potential.

The boss will change and you will be forced to adapt your managing up behaviors to accommodate that new person. Your real job skills, on the other hand, travel with you a lifetime.

Great companies breed independent thinkers—leaders capable of following, not simply complying. There is a fine line that separates the two. At a critical juncture in my career a manager was able to help me recognize that when he paused during a short meeting and said simply, *"Tim, if you and I are always in agreement on every subject then one of us isn't necessary. Push back, challenge me...I need you to help make me better. I need you to help make the company better."*

I never forgot those words.

I've watched leaders and followers struggle to balance those extremes. And I've seen managers who were so enamored with their view of the world that they cultivated legions of EMUs. I also was around for the collapse that inevitably followed. Like a house of cards, teams crafted on managing up are like armies built on the premise of dress inspections. When the battle unfolds, the focus has to be on the enemy—not pleasing the general.

STRAIGHT TALK

It's not complicated. Everyone has to manage up to some degree. Simply recognize that far too many of the Toadies I described in an earlier chapter are often the most culpable in developing the second-level skill of managing up.

Toadies and their first cousins, the EMUs, have a place in organizations, but independent free thinkers are far more valuable in the corporate world.

And the very best leaders know it.

THE BAD BOSS

"A leader is admired, a boss is feared."
~Vicente Del Bosque

Live long enough in corporate and you will encounter the nemesis of career development.

The Bad Boss.

Now before we talk about how you can survive one, let's take the time to dismiss a couple of fallacies that are common when we talk about the subject of bosses.

They include:

> • Our perception of what constitutes a bad boss varies greatly. What I need and what you need will not be the same. And our standards for our manager will be just as different. There is no absolute mold that can be pressed and shipped out from the home office.

> • The tendency to label someone whose style, approach, or character differs from our own as a bad boss is pretty high. The roadways of corporate are littered with the bodies of "wash-outs" who blamed their problems on the person they reported to. More often than not their accusations are woefully misplaced.

> • It is very easy to invest a lot of energy on looking at

the boss and less on ourselves. Just saying.

• Very few *"bosses"* get up each day and think, *"How can I screw somebody's life up today?"* (Well, there may be a few.) The reality is that all of us are consumed with doing what we believe is important; sometimes less so with considering what might be important to others. The message for each of us as followers is equally simple—even bosses may not know what they don't know. What's more, many live in a cocoon that limits their insights, or operate with little to no direction or training for the role they have been asked to assume. This doesn't diminish or excuse poor leadership, but it can sometimes explain some things.

• Know what they call the absolute worst boss in your company today? They call him (or her) boss. The spectrum of performance is not limited to the everyday employee. There are great leaders and there are horrific leaders, and by the luck of the draw if you play the game long enough someday you will draw the short stick.

So, they're out there. And when your day comes, you have choices to make. You can't kill them and still continue your career. That leaves you with three options and three options only:

• Resign

• Transfer

• Learn to live with them

In that vein, here are five **Bad Boss Survival Tips** to consider:

• Ask yourself if you have a clear and relatively unbiased vision of what a great boss should be. A great many are very good at saying what's wrong and far more ambiguous in articulating what should be. Is your vision clear or is it colored by personal feelings?

• Are you prepared to challenge your level of objectivity? You have biases, I have biases, all God's children have biases. Has your opinion been shaped by events that don't allow you to enjoy an accurate picture?

- Have you talked to your boss? Has there been a clear discourse on mutual expectations?

- Do you have a vivid understanding of what great looks like by both of you?

- Is there an agreement on how you will be able to best work together? Remember—it's not a love fest, simply an agreement on how you make this a tenable relationship.

There is no textbook example of how to survive a bad boss. But you can learn from even the worst.

I know—like a lot of other Corporate Survivors I've had my share of mediocre ones to balance against the true greats.

So when your day comes and you find yourself aligned with a Bad Boss it is up to you to decide which of the three options you will pursue. If you decide to make it work then consider the five points outlined above.

Thriving during these leadership voids is a part of almost everyone's career journey even though all of us assume our situation is truly unique. Occasional Bad Bosses are a crisis that is universal.

And like other moments of adversity, it's what you do with the challenge that is most important.

Remember, this too shall pass.

STRAIGHT TALK

The Bad Boss Survivor Tips are battle-tested. Never allow a bad boss to force you out of the company. Sometimes you just have to decide to outlast them.

I can tell you I've done that more than a few times

TORNADO WARNING

"Busy is a drug that a lot of people are addicted to."

~Rob Bell

I still remember the veteran manager who advised me early in my corporate journey that I should expect to meet every example of the human condition in the years ahead, including sociopaths, deviants, and narcissists. Like much of the occasional counsel I received back then I nodded, smiled, and promptly filed it away.

But I will tell you there was a lot of truth to that little prediction (though I would like to think that a representative from the psychopath segment never truly showed up).

At one point in my career I was assigned a special project with a counterpart that was intended to be a one-week commitment. Our responsibilities were clear, as was the time frame. And I knew by the end of our second meeting why some of my colleagues smiled when they saw who I was teamed with. It was one of my first introductions to a personality type I would encounter more than a few times.

The Tornado.

Described as such because they are the true wind creators of the corporate world, and their capacity to compromise organizational effectiveness is at F3 or greater.

My new partner was someone who took the simplest project and transformed it into a four-week ordeal. He literally brought the walls of "things to do" down around us, adding a layer of complexity that compromised our ability to get anything done. I honestly didn't know if he would request maps of the Amazon rain basin or records from the local municipality's traffic court, but it was clear he was intent on justifying the importance of our assignment. And he wanted to make sure everyone knew we were working hard.

By some miracle we got to closure—eventually. And I was offered an incredible learning experience.

The lessons included:

- *"Evidence of effort"* is usually created by a vacuum of leadership. Tornados feed on a simple formula. Let's prove we have value—impress the people above us. Work hard and create a lot of dust.

- Assuming everyone you work with really knows what is most important is a fantasy. It's up to you to define it, and up to you to decide on how to realize it in your plans.

- Clarity of direction and clarity of follow-up is more than just a nice management slogan. Vague assignments without clear outcomes give birth to tornadoes.

- Planning requires some basic skill sets—and you will see them further developed later in the book. The first and most important—the capacity to organize. Without organization, activity for activity's sake takes precedence.

Tornados in the corporate world can find a useful place, but like any strong wind, can also do great damage, particularly if they are in a position of authority.

STRAIGHT TALK

The Phenomenon of the Urgent will be explored in greater detail in a chapter to come. Tornados thrive in the Urgent and they work very hard to pull others into the maelstrom. Your challenge—regardless of whether they are peer, subordinate, or boss—will be in helping them to focus on what's most important.

THE GLASS JAW SYNDROME

"Everybody has a plan until they get hit in the face."
~Mike Tyson

Back in the late '40s and early '50s, a thunderous puncher emerged on the heavyweight boxing scene. His name was Rocky Marciano and he would go on to become the world champion, amassing a stunning 43 knockouts as he marched to an unbeaten 49 victories.

Old-timers say what distinguished Marciano was not so much his power but his ability to take a punch. *"To beat Rocky,"* some said, *"you had to kill him."* Lesser fighters could hit him. It just didn't slow him down.

There are parallels to the corporate jungle. Over the course of your career you will encounter hundreds, perhaps thousands of leaders and peers who are great when they're dictating the action—but amazingly vulnerable when they're on the other side.

In boxing, they have a term for that shortcoming. They call it the *"glass jaw,"* meaning it has a tendency to break when it's tapped very hard. A great many pugilists are world-beaters when they're delivering the blows, but very vulnerable when they're on the other end. And that distinguishes, in many cases, the elite athlete from the also-ran.

The same holds true in the corporate world. Taking a punch here can encompass a lot of things—some of the most noticeable are the ones I call **The Iron Jaw Seven**. They include:

- the ability to offer and to receive feedback;

- the capacity to ask questions—to seek to understand;

- the willingness to entertain differing points of view and, in fact, encourage it;

- the flexibility to change, moderate, or adjust game plans that fall outside of their normal approach;

- the willingness to accept pushback from the people that work for them or with them;

- the drive to stand up when a crisis emerges that threatens them personally and, in those times, to demonstrate what real leadership is all about; and

- the capacity to get off the canvas when knocked down, and use the lessons learned to become even better.

The Flaw of the Glass Jaw is very real and is not limited to those in management positions. I've watched talented performers at every level who grew so enamored with their talents that opposing views couldn't be tolerated. The response was defensiveness, resistance, or outright aggression.

Said another way—they couldn't take a punch.

Want to test this supposition? Ask yourself how many times you have sat in a business meeting, listened to the ramblings of the person in a position of influence, and knew in your heart that what you were hearing was about as off-base as imaginable? Now, how many times have you bitten your tongue—resisted the urge to speak up? Glanced at the eyes of others in the room and seen the same look and knew no one was going to say anything?

If you've been in the business world longer than six months I am going to suggest you have been there. And chances are you are working with someone who has built an environment where disagreement, even productive discourse, has been extinguished.

You are looking at a glass jaw leader. And whether they know it or not, they are limiting the combined genius of the room at large because of their own frailties.

I have worked with thousands of leaders—either for them, with them, or reporting to me.

There are very few Marcianos.

STRAIGHT TALK

You either build your ability to take a punch or you extinguish it by how you interact with others. The very best generally have cultivated two skill sets beyond all others —the capacity to listen and the willingness to respond to the lessons gleaned. There are a lot of posers—not many Iron Jaw Corporate Athletes.

ENEMY MINE

"Do I not destroy my enemies when I make them my friends?"
~Abraham Lincoln

Another reality in the corporate world: Even if you are the nicest, humblest, most magnanimous individual who ever walked the face of the earth you need to embrace this simple notion.

Not everyone is going to like you.

Maybe it's the way you talk, that joke you told back when you were at that meeting six years ago, the report you delivered at last year's conference, or the way you hold a steak knife. It makes no difference why—simply accept the universal tenet that not everyone will embrace you.

In fact, if you're good, really good, you will develop competitors, and yes—even a few internal enemies. It is inevitable. You don't throw people into the arena and expect the adrenaline of competition to lead to group sing-alongs.

Competition yields many positive outcomes, and a few unhealthy ones as well.

One of them is resentment and it is alive and well in many parts of the corporate world. Professional jealousies and allegiances feed it, give it power, and allow it to grow in every company.

I invested the better part of my career trying to treat everyone I met with respect, and I expected no less from others. And I still managed to develop a few adversaries.

It took me some time to understand that how I dealt with them spoke more to my character than some of the easier situations I encountered. It's one thing to have differences—it's another thing to allow them to color how you conduct yourself.

Here are a couple of things I had to learn (and in some cases, the hard way):

• How you treat others—even those you don't particularly care for—will carry with you. In my three-plus decades I raised my voice one time in an interaction with a peer. Oh, there were healthy discussions over those years—don't get me wrong. But only one time where I can say I almost lost my cool, and it involved an individual I believed had lied to me and to others. I let my temper get the better of me and I regretted it. Not because I believed my assumptions about that individual were wrong but because I allowed his behavior to dictate mine. I learned from that.

• You don't have to like everyone, you simply need to be able to work with them. That simple. I've seen really talented people watch their careers take a downturn because they couldn't live and work alongside another person. They allowed it to derail them—compounding the tragedy.

• The best counterbalance to corporate ill will is individual good will. Those who build a legacy of treating others with respect and dignity ultimately win. For every *"enemy"* make certain you have 10 *"advocates."* The numbers will speak for themselves.

• Challenge yourself to look at situations objectively and to remove emotions as best you can. Easy to say—tough to do—but those who can earn a reputation for fairness that will stand the test of time.

STRAIGHT TALK

Reconcile the fact you probably won't become a Career Survivor—or a true leader—without creating some degree of ill will somewhere. It is part of the burden of the role. Accept it and congratulate yourself on the fact that you didn't simply default to cruise control over the course of your career. To affect movement in any organization you have to push things, and that sometimes involves pushing people too. Being an influencer carries with it many costs—and occasionally creating a few people who don't like you may be one of them.

PROCESS

"Over every mountain there is a path, although it may not be seen from the valley."

~Theodore Roethke

Every company has a way of working. And you can bet that it will not necessarily align with the published organizational manual or employee handbook. If you're like most of us it will take time to fully appreciate who owns key decisions and how they're made. And you will struggle to understand how departments really work together versus the company endorsed protocol. In time you will begin to grasp what the lines of accountability are. And more important, you will understand how work is conducted.

Expect to be surprised.

Over the course of my career I've operated in environments where one person could make sweeping decisions and others where five task forces and two committees couldn't agree on what the problem statement was.

You think I'm kidding. I'm not. The callout here is not to demand you become a master of process and systems. It's to recognize that your acumen either will become a career accelerator or a cloying obstruction. As with the other cardinal points of the Compass, how you seek to understand is everything.

THE GAME

"Those against politics are in favor of the politics inflicted upon them."

~Bertolt Brecht

Want to know the people who complain most about politics in the corporate world?

The people who don't know how to play the game.

There is within every company a structure and a way of conducting business, a defined way of how profits are made. And there will always be the intangible brought about by the introduction of the *"people equation"*— the birth of politics.

I admittedly was not the most astute in this area the early part of my career, and so I learned the hard way. But if I could go back now—before the first of the five mergers, the organizational restructures that became too numerous to count, and well before I saw peers sometimes vanish—I might offer these few hard-earned insights. These **Political Survival Tips** would have helped make my life a lot easier:

> • Learn who the influencers are. There is often a difference between those who carry the title and those who have earned the respect. The former may enjoy an official position—the latter wields the weight. Do not assume job title will always be the driver. Who do people listen to? In times of crisis, whom do they reach

out to for context and perspective? Identify them, and more important, get to know them.

• Understand how your business really works, not just how it is supposed to work, and be patient if nothing moves as smoothly as you believe it should. Bureaucracy is one of the first complaints you will hear from corporate newcomers. It is a very real issue in many companies. Your challenge isn't to fix it. It's to successfully navigate it—warts and all.

• Build a sphere of influence, and then add carefully to it as you go. Most of us start work with a group of peers who will have something close to a similar outlook and perhaps even a comparable experience base. As early as you can, find a few allies you can trust. Everyone needs a comrade in his or her foxhole.

• Find a mentor. One who is respected, knowledgeable, and can offer perspective on how your business works. Mentors are a game changer. Ask for their counsel as regards to the points on the Compass—personal accountability, people, processes and perspective. They may not see them as cardinal points but they don't need to—you do. Get their perspective on each—and often.

• Stay above the fray. Emotions and pettiness can reign in the corporate world. If you can retain your calm—even when the bullets are flying—your chances for survival increase exponentially. Recognize that your real challenge is in forging a valued presence that legitimizes your role. Let the others dip low. Stay above.

• Keep your eye on the prize. You were hired or promoted into your role for a reason. That reason ties back to a business objective. You're not in the corporate world to build cliques, establish a settlement, or to endlessly compete with every other employee. The best recognize the opposition is outside the company walls—the firm fighting yours for market dominance.

• Take the time to learn the ropes, not simply rail
against them. OK, your company has political issues
and you've stubbed your toe a few times. Big deal.
You're not the first and you won't be the last. Learn
from it. Move on.

STRAIGHT TALK

Politics are a part of life. And yet there are still people who
overcome. Adversity is a part of your climb. You have three
choices: complain, leave, or adapt. Take a guess which one a
majority of survivors select.

DOPPLER DOWN

*"You can find something truly important
in an ordinary minute."*

~Mitch Albom

Some people create their own storms and then rant when they start to get wet. I see it every day.

A few years back my wife and I decided to install motion detector lights at the back of our house. They weren't very costly and since I spent time on the road it provided a greater sense of security for her when I was away.

They worked great. Every bit of movement in our backyard activated them: every dog, every cat, every raccoon, every field mouse, every puff of wind, swaying tree branch, or falling acorn—everything. We quickly learned the motion detectors were pretty non-discriminating. And by the third night no one paid too much attention when the lights activated.

Maybe there was merit in paying more for those lights, but I doubt it. Everything clicked them on.

There are parallels between the motion detectors and our professional lives.

We are each outfitted with our own version of that same light, and if we're not careful they are constantly clicking *"on."* In many cases it's because we can't discriminate between idle movement and the few things that warrant our real time and attention.

Any movement activates our sensors.

James Murphy's book, *Flawless Execution*, talks about the insidious effects of a phenomenon he calls task saturation. Simply stated, it suggests when we overload on making everything important we effectively make nothing important. He offers multiple examples of organizations becoming so overwhelmed with *"stuff"* they fail to land the plane, offering a real-world example of where disproportionate attention on the trivial resulted in airline disaster.

In the corporate world the enemy of productivity has a name. It's called The Storm.

The battering effect of the *"to dos"* often dominate our lives. Like that swaying tree branch in my backyard, we click "on" with the latest email missive or when that new meeting request crosses our desk. The storm represents all the distractions that rob of us of true effectiveness. Over time, it often results in the corporate equivalent of Attention Deficit Disorder—the mad rush from crisis to crisis—and its symptoms can be devastating.

I help build the storm and am responsible for the disease. Chances are good you are too. In the murky world of Corporate ADD we struggle to focus on what's most important on a daily basis, and the default is universal—at least do something. And so we pass on the malady.

The scary part of the storm is it is often difficult to comprehend its causes and sometimes, when you're in the middle of it, you don't even know it. We are like the walking zombies in those horror movies, plodding along in a slow death march, blinded by the winds.

There are four dimensions in the corporate world that should dictate where you invest your time and effort. Remember them because whether you like it or not, they are very real:

> • The first is the Unimportant and Not Urgent. In that bucket you can place a lot of things that could be done but don't demand your immediate attention. And anytime you bear witness to the mindless computer games that occupy co-workers' time you're probably seeing a good example. See also: office betting pools, political debates, and football game debriefs. Not everything we do in our corporate lives is truly mission critical. In some companies this one bucket can constitute much time and attention.

• The second is the Unimportant and Urgent. The great black hole for many. Our motion detector kicks in and we are compelled to take action because a deadline demands it and/or another email just crossed our screen. Circle this box in red— it's the single greatest suck on our time and energy.

• The third is the Important and Not Urgent. Critical to the business but easy to put on the backburner—and procrastinate around. Want to bet where energy that could be invested here is often spent? See Unimportant and Urgent.

• The last is the Important and Urgent. Where our time must be invested if we want to stay employed. Ignore this bucket at your own peril.

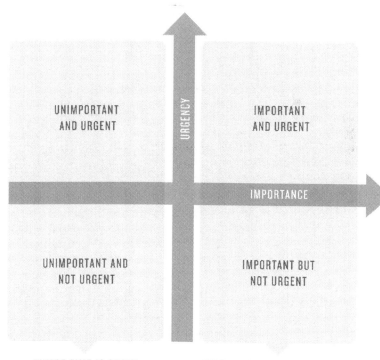

WHERE TIME IS SPENT   WHERE TIME SHOULD BE SPENT

The above compartments were first defined by Peter Drucker when the corporate world was much simpler. It's said that Dwight Eisenhower made them a cornerstone of how he managed his life. Their value is exponentially more important today. The rise of technology has carried with it the ominous emergence of what I call the Big U Urgent—and the Big U doesn't take any prisoners when it comes to dominating our lives.

Why? Because the Big U often shows up masquerading as Important. It looks Important and it tastes Important. And like my old motion detector, we are hardwired to respond to it. But remember that more information crosses our paths today than at any other time in human history. We are bombarded with emails, text messages careen across our phone, and deadlines emerge from our very pores. The stimuli can be overwhelming.

The Big U is very, very real.

It also can and often does represent the gusts of the storm that create Corporate ADD. But the Big U is not always critical to your business.

So, in a perfect world, where should our time be invested?

The Important—the third and fourth buckets above.

Easily said, isn't it?

But distinguishing the Important is very difficult for most. It requires skills that many don't take the time to develop—they simply act. And so they fall victim to the Big U.

There are core steps you can take that can help you find sanctuary from the storm and to survive Corporate ADD. And even after all these years believe me when I say I still sometimes struggle to live these principles in my own life. It's much easier to just submit to the comforting siren of the gales.

The motion detector won't get you there. Not every movement demands action on your part. Like your local weatherperson you need a refined system to separate the cloyingly Urgent from what is truly Important. Your personal Doppler radar has to differentiate the light showers from the dangerous storms.

If your Doppler is down then every movement in your area of the world will trigger a response. I've watched a lot of colleagues swept away in the wash.

STRAIGHT TALK

Learning to organize your tasks is an important first step for any Career Survivor. But it's only when you begin to then prioritize those tasks that you start to take control of the storm—and that means differentiating the Important from the Urgent.

But these two core skills are only the first steps. Read on.

A CURE FOR
CORPORATE ADD

*"The battle for our hearts is fought
on the pages of our calendar."*

~Bob Goff

Tomorrow morning a great percentage of employees in the corporate world will walk into their job feeling stressed and overwhelmed. Their *"to do"* list is expanding and their *"can do"* is declining, even as the next demand is placed on their shoulders. And they'll leave their place of work feeling worse.

Here's another plain talk chapter and I hope you will read it carefully. I'm going to destroy a few myths here. They include:

- the notion that multi-tasking is an essential job skill in the corporate world;

- the illusion of time management; and

- the assumption that highly organized people are always the most effective.

One of the best investments I ever made was the purchase of a day planner in my early days in the corporate world. It seemed logical; I saw others who carried them and they looked professional, and in those days anything that I thought added to the *"look"* had to help.

But it took me all of about two weeks to learn that planning was more than a cosmetic addition in my approach to my new role. It was going to be a difference maker that would either save me or facilitate my downfall.

I was in new waters and in a world where if you didn't drive results you simply didn't stay long. That simple.

Planning to that point had extended to occasionally using a calendar to track meetings or social commitments. I was not a natural planner or inherently organized.

But I learned to be. And in time the ability to compartmentalize my work assignments, and to plan how I approached them, not only made me more effective—it became an amazing stress reliever. I began to appreciate the power of organization.

But it wasn't enough. I could move thick piles of highly organized stuff but still dealt with the frustration of too much to do. Which led me to a far more important skill set—the ability to prioritize.

Prioritizing on an hourly, daily, weekly, or even monthly basis is a different animal. Most of us group things easily enough, but truly deciding what is most important in our lives can be troubling. If you can't prioritize, you can't manage your time. If you can't manage your time and your energy, you will play catch up from Day One.

I can remember the first highly organized manager I ever reported to. Every day you could walk into his office and see what he had decided was most important that day—his list fully written out. He was the first I ever worked with who did one more thing—he distinguished the difference between Important and Urgent. And I found that to be extraordinary. I had come up toiling under the assumption that the best corporate players constantly juggled their tasks. And yet, here was a highly successful executive who pursued "solo-tasking" with a passion. He didn't run from fire to fire—he made his *"to do"* list his guide. And I began to understand multi-tasking wasn't so much a corporate skill as it was often a failure to prioritize where time and energy should be devoted.

It was the beginning of a foundation that would eventually form my **Planning Golden Three**—the best way to effectively cure the perpetual state of anxiety that typifies the victims of Corporate Attention Deficit Disorder. The steps below are easy to understand. Your challenge will be in demonstrating the discipline required to actually put them into play in your life.

Step 1—Get **Organized.** Specifically:

- Purchase a planner and take the steps to learn how to

use it—and that tool can be electronic or manual. The actual device is less important than what you do with it.

• Group similar work assignments into categories in that planner. Don't just rely on expansive "to do" lists. Like a room cluttered with stuff, so to is your business life if you simply collect things. Build a degree of order—every day. Without it you can't optimize your effectiveness.

• Find a way to combine your meeting notes with your planner and your calendar. Ideally, one vehicle that becomes your "go-to" source. I've written out every note for every meeting, project, or assignment I've participated in for my entire career. Old school? Maybe, but then again I have a working archive—a journal that captures my experiences that continues to teach me.

• You should have some defined method to capture key notes and, perhaps most important, to time-activate those points that require action for every meeting you ever attend. I have always been amazed at how often people discuss Actionable Items or follow up, and then nothing takes place after. A well-constructed planner can help make sure you hold up your end of the bargain.

Step 2—Learn how to **Prioritize**. Specifically:

• Acknowledge they're not making any more minutes on Monday. Same for Tuesday and every other day of the week. Time management implies a resource you can adjust, expand, or remodel to fit your unique needs. Like oceanfront property, they aren't making any more minutes. Your challenge is to manage your energy for maximum return. You do that when you carefully distinguish where that energy will be invested. Time management is a catchy term but it is a misnomer.

• Learn to differentiate between the Urgent and the Important. The latter ties to your primary goals and whether that's business or personal, if you invest your time there you optimize your effectiveness.

• Beware the potential black hole of electronic

communication, including email, Twitter, Instagram, and every other variation on the above that is either out there or on the way. Yes, technology is great but without discipline information overload can complicate rather than simplify our lives. Remember the Big U often comes disguised as Important.

• Make certain you invest at least 15 minutes every morning in reviewing your key activities for the day. Develop some type of method to prioritize that list. Decide what is most important and make that your mission. I routinely use a 4-star, 3-star, 2-star, 1-star method to designate what and where I will devote my energy. And yes, the stars match up with the four boxes discussed earlier. The 4 is the Urgent and Important, the 3 is the Not Urgent and Important, the 2 is the Urgent and Unimportant, and the 1 is the Not Urgent and Unimportant. You would be correct if you assume the 4-star items are must dos, the 3-star items I plan for in the near term, the 2-star items I may either delegate or push into the schedule down the line, and the 1 star I address only if I find myself with time to spare. At the end of day I invest 15 minutes to make sure I have fully formed the next day's plans.

Step 3—**Calendarize**

• The missing piece for most—if you have prioritized what's most important it is essential for you to then schedule the time to commit to that priority. Literally go into your calendar and block the time. Every 4 star and 3 star should be calendarized. Every day—for the rest of your professional life.

• Effectively budget your day, your week, and your month according to how you have prioritized your life. And make that commitment one you live by.

• Control your calendar—completely. It will either be dictated by your priorities or it will be dictated by those around you. Don't concede the power of energy management. Budget time according to what you consider most important. Specifically:

- Make certain you can review and reject meetings based on need, not others' assumptions of need.
- Overlay the Important with your schedule—every day. The 4- and 3-star priorities dictate where you invest your time.

Pretty simple, and yet less than one in 20 will apply the principles and they will continue to struggle—long-term victims of Corporate Attention Deficit Disorder.

One of the best books I've read on the subject of true energy management is Kevin Kruse's *15 Secrets Successful People Know About Time Management*—a must for those committed to optimizing their life.

STRAIGHT TALK

The Planning Golden Three represents a proven formula that has allowed me to survive in the corporate world:

- (O) Organize by using tools and tactics that ensure you can clearly look at your life.
- (P) Prioritize by carefully distinguishing the difference between the Urgent and the Important—every day and every hour.
- (C) Calendarize by making certain your Important becomes a part of your daily, weekly, and monthly schedule.

Three simple steps—master them and you've built a foundation that will allow you to survive. OPC—**the cure for Corporate ADD.**

THE CORE ANALYTICS

"Clarity affords focus."

~Thomas Leonard

There is a reality you will want to be mindful of: as your scope of responsibility grows, someone above is going to want to know you have your act together.

At some point in your career you will be introduced to what most companies call an Action Plan Update; the requirement to demonstrate to your firm you have an idea of how you will accomplish what you're paid to do. There are dozens of names different companies use for these updates (Pulse Checks, Mini-Briefings, Progress Overviews, etc.). You get the picture—the intent is to quickly and easily communicate what's important to the person or persons you report to.

Here is a simple approach that might help you begin to consider how to demonstrate your expertise early on. I've used it for 30 years. It's never failed to help me get to the core of what needed to be communicated—and it gave me a great foundation on which to build my story.

I'm not sure where I was first introduced to what I call The Core Analytics but I can't take credit for its development. Like many ideas shared in this book I have benefited from a great many people who touched my life and from articles, books, and other resource pieces I sought out on my own.

The premise here is remarkably straightforward. Whether you manage a project, a business unit, or the department intramural team, there are very basic questions that you need to be able to answer about your corner of the world. Their impact can be powerful.

The key questions:

> • **Where am I?** This asks us to honestly assess what is the "state of the union" of the business we manage. Is it succeeding? Why or why not?
>
> • **How did I get there?** What were the plans you had in place to get to here? What are the core activities that carried you to your current state? Were they the right tactics? Why or why not?
>
> • **Where do I want to be?** Now some of the magic begins to take hold. We talked earlier about the notion of goals and objectives and their importance in career planning. The same holds true for your Action Plan Update. If you cannot articulate in simple terms where you think you should be, then forget all the steps that came before—and all the ones that come after. By the way, you would be surprised to see how difficult it is for most businesspeople to succinctly answer the three questions I've just outlined.
>
> • **How will I get there?** No goal or objective is any more than a dream if there isn't a specific recitation of key actions that comes after. This is where you advance to strategy and tactics (the how behind your game plan.) Here you move beyond broad statements of where you think you should be and challenge yourself to articulate a clear plan.
>
> • **What results should I expect and when?** No plan is complete without milestones or key measures you've identified that will outline whether you're making progress —or simply treading water.

The above five questions are not intended to represent a full Action Plan Update. They are intended to offer you a quick and easy guide on which to build. Answer them succinctly and you greatly accelerate your chances of survival when you're called to speak to your portion of the business.

Together, they provide a framework for your personal narrative. But The Core Analytics will not guarantee you success. More is required than a simple recitation of the data and the facts if you want to make a difference in your company. And it took me a very long time to really understand that. The Power of Story in an upcoming chapter will make that very clear.

EVERY TIME
YOU SIT DOWN

"It is never too late to be what you might have been."

~George Eliot

Performance evaluations.

Some in the corporate world argue they are the bane of true performance enhancement. Formal, systematized, and driven at times by Human Resource departments more concerned with company-approved guidelines deemed legally defensible than in truly differentiating top talent and motivating employees to perform.

A fair and equitable Performance Evaluation process is not easy to build or to administer. Some years ago I was fortunate enough to develop a system for one of our legacy companies that was used for over a half dozen years. I can safely say I learned that no matter how much time and attention is devoted to its creation, there is no perfect approach to assessing people's skills and overall contributions.

But there are a couple of outputs that resonated for me. Again—tips from a Corporate Survivor you might consider. And those tips begin with one very simple notion.

Your Performance Review is not something done to you. It's something you should be prepared to lead through.

Here's a list of inalienable rights and responsibilities you should consider if you are going to maximize your contributions—and yes, the individual performance reviews to come. **The Corporate Survivor Performance Review Ten Commandments** include:

- Thou shalt make certain you know the expectations for your job. Sounds stupid, doesn't it? That should be fairly intuitive. Don't kid yourself; your interpretation of what your role is and your manager's will likely be different, sometimes radically different. It's been my experience that there is usually a lot of misinterpretation. You can't afford that. Sit down and discuss what is expected. Ask questions. Make sure you have a clear vision of what great looks like. The number one reason people fail—they don't know what it is they are supposed to do. And the other reasons are far behind.

- Thou shalt make sure you understand how you will be trained. And if your answers to the bulleted point above don't align with the training that will be provided, ask how the gaps will be addressed. Companies are sometimes very clear in saying what they expect but much more ambiguous in providing the hands-on training needed to help you do the job. Without the training you are being set up for failure.

- Thou shalt take ownership in soliciting and in receiving feedback, and do it as early and as often as possible. Challenge your manager to offer it even if they are uncomfortable in providing it. It's your career. You either drive it or you are a passive reactor. Take the steering wheel.

- Thou shalt ask for as many examples of excellence as you can handle, either through your manager or via your peers. It's hard to demonstrate outstanding performance if you don't know what it looks like to begin with.

- Thou shalt take notes when the subject of performance arises. Too many people fly by the seat of their pants. Don't be one of them.

- Thou shalt determine your performance evaluation

is something you can heavily influence if you choose. But to do that requires your taking an active role in your own development. Unfortunately, most are passive recipients. Wrong approach. Every formal meeting with your manager/supervisor/leader should include some degree of discussion around how you're tracking on performance. Someone told me once, "Every time you sit down, you should know where you stand." Pretty sage advice.

• Thou shalt call out early on that you expect to be a top performer. Engage your managers in that undertaking. Challenge them (and yes, you will hear that term repeatedly when we talk about performance evaluations) to help you get there. Let them know you hold them just as accountable for an outstanding review as they hold you. Bold? Yes, but I will guarantee you those few who set the bar high for themselves and do the same thing with their managers set a tone that will serve them well later.

• Thou shalt document your successes. Make that a dynamic record that you can, at a moment's notice, provide to your manager. Use it to populate the self-assessment portion of your Mid- and End of Year review. The alternative is Creative Writing 101—the mindless search to justify your greatness and to meet the timeline for your review.

• Thou shalt never pass on the opportunity to comment in writing on your review. That electronic summary is a legal document. It can dictate your next promotion, your salary increase, and yes, your job security. It is a lot more than a simple letter. Treat it as such.

• Thou shalt retain every Performance Review you receive and plan to reference those documents as a potential Free Agent for the rest of your professional life. Again—no proof of performance equals no performance in the eyes of a prospective employer.

And if you're in a formal leadership position, a few things to consider as you assess the people who report to you:

- Spend the time to do it right. I've seen far too many managers who gloss over the process or attach a number rating and then move on after a half hour of completing a spreadsheet. I've even read Performance Reviews that were basically generic with slight tweaks for everyone on the team. That's an insult to your people.

- Differentiate your talent. The greatest single step you can take toward company mediocrity is when you group everyone in the middle. Top performers will see it, they will resent it, and the very best will not tolerate it.

- Be specific and be behaviorally based in your comments. No one cares about your feelings nor do they want to hear generalities around their personality traits. If you can't offer a specific example you can't provide quality feedback.

- Avoid the inherent biases that can afflict leaders. We tend to reward persons with similar backgrounds, belief systems, and approaches to the job. A major mistake.

STRAIGHT TALK

Whether you are a follower or a supervisor, every time you sit down you should know where you stand.

THE MEETING MAZE

*"Meetings are indispensible
when you don't want to do anything."*

~John Kenneth Galbraith

When you were a kid you had a lot of things that kept you from your homework—the baseball game down the street, the latest video game you just had to play, the NFL game your dad and you were going to watch, or maybe that budding romance that demanded your attention.

You name it. There were distractions (some welcomed, some not) that occasionally kept you from what you should be doing.

News flash—you haven't seen distractions yet.

When you enter the corporate world a whole new series of disruptive factors will rob you of time, energy, and attention. They include, but are not limited to, technology and all its trappings, social commitments, conflicting professional priorities, and, oh yes—meetings.

Let's be clear, meetings serve an essential purpose in your new world. They're where we align our efforts, check for consensus, assess progress, debate and arrive at key action plans, and build coalitions. The list is long and the value indisputable.

Why then will you arrive at the conclusion so many do that a significant percentage of meetings are a total and complete waste of time?

Here's five **No Meeting Guidelines** you might consider as either someone who schedules meetings or as a participant requested to attend. Maybe somewhere down the line one of them will give you back at least a small portion of your life:

• No meeting without a clear objective should be attended. They may call it goals, outputs, or projected outcomes but regardless of the jargon it's wrapped in— no reason for being there, no attendance.

• No meeting without Actionable Items that emerge as a result warrants your time. Unless it's a general discussion to gain feedback or opinion you have to ask, "If the participants aren't going to do anything different as a result of their investment of time, why are they there?"

• No meeting should take place without a defined time frame. Work expands to fill the seconds, minutes, and hours that's accorded it. The "let's get together to discuss our business" is an invitation to slip into a black hole. Don't go there.

• No meeting should take place without a clear leader responsible for the objectives and agenda. That leader should make certain they either manage the clock or delegate someone to.

• No meeting that doesn't ultimately advance your business warrants being held.

THANK YOU, MAM

"Integrity is telling myself the truth.
And honesty is telling the truth to other people."
~Spencer Johnson

Since we're keeping it real here, let's put one more thing about meetings on the table. Everyone knows about it but it's seldom discussed.

It's the "other" meeting—the one that follows the real meeting, only without the company spiel attached. You know—the water cooler debrief, the lunchroom conclave, the breakfast club chatter, the texter's hotline. When participants gather to talk about what "they really think"—minus the Corporate Political Correctness.

I call them MAMs (Meetings after the Meeting) and they are as real as corporate strategies, mission statements, performance reviews, and balance sheets.

Depending on your company, your division, or your department, MAMs can be a powerful adjunct to your company's strategy or one of the most disruptive counters to real progress.

The challenge for every employee is to find a way to take the MAMs into the light of day; to get the real issues that people want to talk about to a forum where they can be discussed productively.

Not easy to do. And let's understand that not every MAM member wants resolution. There are, in every company, the cynical few—the vipers— who can and sometimes do make up what I call the vocal minority. MAMs offer them a ready-made venue to spout their venom. Many of them would never want their platforms wasted away by real action. The vipers are easy to recognize. They will find the ugliness in a rainbow and the danger in a butterfly.

Want to increase your chances of corporate survival? Find a way to limit your contact with the vipers. There is more at play in their unhappiness than where they choose to go to work.

Let's get to the real issue; taking MAMs into a forum where opportunities, solutions, problems, and issues can actually be talked about, not shuffled into dark corners.

There's a way, but it's dependent on these **Anti-MAM Measures**:

> • Leaders who are willing to listen. One of the best I ever worked with practically demanded team members to call out gaps, to challenge on where we could be better as a company; or where he could be more effective as a leader. He sometimes asked, "So, what are people going to talk about out there?" He would point toward the hallway and add, "That we should instead talk about in here?" Think that reinforced transparency?

> • Followers who are willing to lead. Courage is an underappreciated characteristic of top performing individuals and top performing companies. In every group there has to be at least a few willing to step up and offer the unspoken obvious. I call it being 25 percent more honest. Courage begets courage. Others watch and yes, they will follow.

> • A willingness on everyone's part to entertain opposing views. I can't count the number of times that a perceived problem, one that would have simmered had it not made its way to a public forum, turned out not to be much of an issue at all. It's amazing how often a group will actually call out and help others differentiate between private gripes and what are real obstacles to success. And yes, vipers generally hate the illumination this can provide. It's a lot easier to stay in the shadows and hiss.

> • A commitment to act. Nothing encourages

transparency more than seeing your suggestions take flight. Nothing. Most of the people who are most unhappy in a company are the ones who feel they have no power, no influence, and no future.

• Recognition and reward for the quiet heroes. I've seen leaders who went out of their way to acknowledge individuals who took steps to take the MAMs public. By reinforcing this simple Best Practice, others were made more willing to take ownership in their business. The impact was exponential.

STRAIGHT TALK

MAMs never die. Nor should they in a free society. But a company's willingness and ability to bring their narrative back into productive forums—not just whispers in a hallway—can often separate the great from the good.

CAREER INFARCTS

"Human genius has its limits while human stupidity does not."
~Alexandre Dumas, fils

I watched my friend weave his way in the direction of the microphone, wobbling slightly as he reached over one of the other guests to grab it away. And then he turned to face the hundreds of people gathered in the banquet hall.

He was stone-cold drunk, angry, and the center of his frustrations—the division's lead—was seated some 15 feet away.

And then my friend effectively ended his own career.

You spend enough time on the corporate trail and you will inevitably witness or certainly hear about what I refer to as career infarcts.

Infarct, by definition, refers to the sudden occlusion of oxygen or blood flow to a vessel or organ, stimulating tissue loss or death. I borrow the term from the medical field, but it is a phenomenon not limited to just the cardiovascular system.

The blunders that precede certain professional death happen every day in the corporate world.

Your ability to last in this jungle you must navigate will depend on how well you recognize and respond to warnings or danger signals before you become a victim.

Here are several **Career Infarct Accelerators**. I've watched each of them end promising futures:

- Alcohol flows freely at meetings and social affairs and there is a fine line between socially imbibing and trouble. Your business is your business. Your social life is your social life. Don't confuse the two. And if you're in your first 10 years post-college do not assume the after-dinner company gathering is just like the days of the fraternity *"kegger."* It's not.

- The Meeting after the Meeting (MAM) that deteriorates into a public forum—and a self-administered death sentence. You are always on company time to a certain degree. Every digital message leaves a footprint—forever. You want to express your views—that's fine. But understand that there could be repercussions. Use common sense.

- Tempers and egos—important character traits that all of us are equipped with. Of the two, the most potentially damaging is the latter but both can and will create problems in the corporate world, particularly for those with relatively low Emotional Quotients (EQs). My best advice, recognize when your inner voice suggests either is about to spiral out of control and then remove yourself and collect your wits. The friend I mentioned at the beginning of this chapter literally ended his career because of his distaste for the person in power caused him to enter into an unrehearsed "roast" at a company banquet. His 20- plus years of service terminated because of five minutes of stupidity.

- Affairs of the heart can cripple a career and yes, I've witnessed my share of counterparts who allowed them to do just that. It can be challenging working alongside people you may develop a more than professional interest in, but if you choose to go there, recognize you are potentially setting yourself up for more than typical heartache. And I won't even begin to speak to relationships in the same department or within a reporting line. Deadly.

• Administrative malfeasance carries an ominous tone and it should. I'm not sure I can effectively count the number of people I've encountered over the years who saw their careers end because of "stupid stuff." I'm talking hedging on their expense reports, violating company protocols, trying to skirt guidelines, or faking their activity. I've sat in meetings where individuals who—had they spent as much time doing their job as they did in trying to falsify their records—could have been superstars. Instead they lost their employment. Honesty is not a difficult concept, but I continue to be amazed at how often otherwise intelligent people choose to compromise it.

• Failure to do what's required. It's a lesson I first began to appreciate from an article in the Harvard Business Review 30 years ago, but it remains timeless. A great many people go to work each day not clear on what it is they are supposed to do. When people hear that they often shake their heads and say, *"That doesn't apply to me though."* Want to check that supposition? Tomorrow, ask your manager to articulate what he or she thinks are the most important core skills of your role and what they hold you accountable for. Before you ask the question write down your answers to them. Over half the time your answers will differ greatly—over half the time. Why? Because most companies don't invest the time to really consider roles and responsibilities; instead they farm out job documentation to Human Resources. If you have never had the frank dialogue with your manager about mutual expectations for the position you currently hold, join the rest of the corporate world. It doesn't happen nearly as often as you might imagine.

I'm reminded of an article I read once about ex-San Francisco 49ers' football coach Bill Walsh, who led that team to multiple Super Bowl championships. When Walsh took the helm of the team he took the time to rewrite the job docs for every position on the team— every assistant coach, every player role, every locker room worker—everybody. When asked why, his answer was beautifully simple. He explained he could do it on the front end or spend his time later trying to outline for team members what he truly expected. He chose to do it before performance rather than backpedaling after.

• Failure to adapt. Our ability to perpetually reinvent ourselves is crucial to longevity in the corporate world. It's not necessarily the strongest that survive; it's the ones most adaptable to change who last—who prosper.

STRAIGHT TALK

Career infarcts are very real. There are healthy choices you can make to minimize your risk, but a great many ignore them until they are at crisis stage. It's your decisions that dictate your future.

PERSPECTIVE

"It's not what you look at that matters, it's what you see."
~Henry David Thoreau

I never thought of myself as biased in my thinking or blatantly narrow-minded in how I approached either my life or my job. In fact, I prided myself on my objectivity, until I began to appreciate that my definition of objectivity was forged by beliefs that weren't always defensible.

Especially when my paycheck and my future were involved.

In the chapters that follow I'll offer context for taking the broader view of your corporate journey and share a few tips I learned about better understanding yourself.

Personal Accountability offers you consistent direction for your career. Understanding and mastering the nuances of People and Process gives you lift. But it is Perspective that is the faculty that will keep you on course for a lifetime. When honed, it can drive your career. When dulled or allowed to grow toxic, it can kill.

THE TALE OF THE
TWO CHARLIES

"The years teach much which the days never knew."

~Ralph Waldo Emerson

I go to great lengths not to use real names in this book. Though the people and the events are all based on my experiences, I don't tie them back to any one person or persons.

Not so for this chapter. Two men had a profound impact on my career, even though the sum of my interactions with each could be counted in minutes, not hours. For very different reasons they offered me insight I carried with me three-plus decades.

Maybe some of what they said will have value for you.

The first Charlie was a man who was my next-door neighbor for at least a portion of my youth. He worked at a bank for years before he went into the pharmaceutical business and moved away. My parents always talked about how successful he had become and I knew only that he lived over in the country club section of the little town I grew up in. That was good enough for me.

I didn't see much of him after I reached the age of 12, only heard about him. He was a businessman and everybody knew Charlie had money. Then, on a weekend trip back home shortly after I went into pharmaceuticals, I happened to run across him downtown. Charlie had grown older, gray now but certainly recognizable, and was seated on a city bench talking with the owner of the local record store (yes, we still had record stores as late as the early '80s). I reintroduced myself and he was thrilled to hear about my good fortune. By then Charlie had invested over 20 years in the corporate world, and I could tell he wanted to hear about my company and the sales position I had taken on. We spent five minutes catching up and reliving memories of the old neighborhood until I wished him well and excused myself, finally heading back across the street to my car.

"Tim, come back," Charlie yelled, *"I got something I want to tell you."*

I returned and he motioned for me to lean closer. He said in a low voice six words I would never forget. *"Don't let them bleed you dry."*

I paused and then smiled back at him.

"I mean it," he continued. *"If you let them, companies will bleed you dry."*

I thanked him and walked away, figuring old Charlie had spent too much time on that damn bench.

Four years later I was moving into my first management role with the company. I had advanced through several sales positions, won an award or two, and managed to establish myself as something of a fast-tracker. In June of my fifth year I attended my first managers meeting along with some 50 leaders from around the country who bore responsibility for our sales team. Our keynote speaker at that meeting was our outgoing vice president of sales. This Charlie was a 30-year veteran who had been cajoled into returning (after a planned retirement three years before) to lead our company through one of its first great growth spurts. Now, after reaching a plateau that allowed him to finally pursue a retirement long dreamed about, he was taking a few minutes at the end of the meeting to share the lessons of a lifetime.

I sat five rows back and dutifully took notes, but my mind was racing about the district meetings to come and the prep work in making sure they were seamless. These first meetings with my new team had to be razor sharp. But somewhere during his comments, Charlie's words began to sink in—if only a little bit.

I heard a man that day who wanted to speak about something far more important than the latest marketing strategy or sales numbers. There was a measure of sincerity—maybe even sadness—that I had never heard before.

Charlie wanted to tell us there was more to life than this game of business. He wanted to tell us that matters of family, of faith, and of friends should always be placed in a higher position. I didn't know it at the time but Charlie's health was not the greatest and he profoundly regretted decisions he had made to not spend more time with his loved ones.

"You have to take the time to smell the roses," he said. *"Before you know it, they're gone."* And there was a tiny break in his voice as he continued: *"I know because I sometimes failed to do that."*

Charlie was arguably the most successful man I had ever really talked to. He led a sales force. My guess was he was a millionaire and I know now he was—several times over. He helped lead the growth of one of the most amazing pharmaceutical companies in the '70s and early '80s, but he sounded remarkably like someone who had learned late in life a more important lesson.

Four years later Charlie was dead. I heard about his demise in a short company email that outlined his many contributions and thanked him for the sacrifices made.

In the years that followed, the young man who sat in the room that day and acknowledged but maybe didn't really hear Charlie's words came to appreciate their poignancy.

The two Charlies gave me a wonderful gift—true perspective.

STRAIGHT TALK

Embrace the corporate game and your career with passion and with vigor. But understand that it is a game—and like any game, it is meant to be played.

But if the game becomes your life then you can be assured of only one thing.

You've already lost.

MIRROR, MIRROR ON THE WALL

"Life is only a reflection of what we allow ourselves to see."
~Trudy Vesotsky

All of us enter our professional lives with our own individual set of skills, experiences, philosophies, and educational backgrounds. Add to that the attitudes and values that make us truly unique. The result of this is that we all carry around two self-issued pieces of vital equipment on our journeys. Everyone gets the same two pieces, yet each is unique.

Whether and how you learn to use them is pretty much up to you, but they are allocated to all of us.

The first is a magnifying glass. Through that lens you will look out at the rest of the world. It might provide you with understanding, context, and even dimension on your surroundings. If you're like most of us, it will be a fairly large piece of equipment, sometimes to the point of being burdensome.

The second is a mirror. Through that you will be able to look at yourself. Assume it will be fairly tiny.

Fit in your shirt pocket tiny.

You'll carry these two tools whether you recognize it or not. They are there. And they have been with you since birth.

What no one will tell you is that the lens on both of these pieces is flawed, sometimes terribly so. It will be up to you to figure out the reasons for the flaws.

Together they can create a laser focus on your world. Or they can lead you to develop myopia that will leave you blind—and to a level of self-absorption that can derail your career.

Long before the term Emotional Intelligence (EQ) became popular, I had begun to realize how flawed the lens I looked out at the world—my magnifying glass—really was. And the one I used to examine myself—my mirror—suffered equal distortions.

I remember walking into a national sales meeting in the early '80s on the heels of a record-breaking personal sales year, my first in the institutional division. I had enjoyed a promotion from my field representative role and had finished the year as the number one in percentage of quota in the country. My manager greeted my wife and me and had tipped us off that a national award was likely coming my way.

We were ecstatic, and on the day of the awards ceremony I found a place in the front row of that giant banquet hall, the better to hear the glowing accolades that would soon be coming my way as that year's *"champion of champions"* was introduced to the sales organization. I still remember my heart pounding as the speaker began to describe my incredible accomplishments and as I struggled to remember the *"impromptu remarks"* I had so carefully planned when I accepted.

Right up to the point that someone else was announced as the winner.

I was devastated as I watched a far more senior peer take "my award." I looked over to my manager and watched him look back at me with an apologetic shrug and a sheepish grin.

This must be some kind of ridiculous mistake, I told myself. They just gave that guy my award.

Granted, he had produced for multiple years versus my single year in the division, but I was number one. I deserved that award. Or so I told myself.

My magnifying glass—flaws and all—was at a red-hot level. Only it was so huge and blurred by my emotion that I couldn't really see. If I had I would have understood the winner had built 10-plus years of excellence, and the latest was just a continuation of that pattern. And I would have appreciated that the flaws of goal-making made it much more difficult for a sales rep to repeat—or three-peat—or in his case, 10-peat.

He had.

And my mirror? Well, my mirror was at full self-deception mode and teeny-tiny. I was drinking my own personal version of the Kool-Aid, with an IV hooked up alongside to hurry the intoxication process.

But as emotions cooled, I was able to take the time to learn from the experience; and the more I reflected on it the more I realized the right decision had been made—even though it wasn't the outcome I had hoped for.

And though I committed to removing any doubt about award-worthy performance in the future, the larger lesson was the insight the experience offered me.

I began to appreciate that my ability to more objectively interpret how I looked at the world around me must continue to evolve. More important, I needed to be prepared to ask myself the tough questions that allowed me to better look at myself.

I had work to do—a lot of work. And it began with a magnifying glass that was clouded by my own self-interest and a mirror that had so inflated my head that I couldn't see. I'm not sure but I've often wondered if it was one of the more important insights of my career.

Is anyone's lens perfect?

Maybe, but I haven't met them yet.

It's been my experience that a majority of us invest an incredible amount of time and energy examining the shortcomings of the world that surrounds us, but very little assessing ourselves. It's what gives rise to the infamous "us and them" divider that can corrupt companies.

It's easier to look out than to look in. I know—my magnifying glass is still pretty heavy.

But I think it's the mirror that we can use to transform. That's the resource that helps us embrace and ultimately develop a critical Corporate Survivor Core Skill—accountability for our actions. To build accountability we have to be prepared to look into that mirror and ask ourselves tough questions.

More important, we must be prepared to answer.

I didn't win that award because I was a short-term *"wonder,"* like the NFL player who flashes and then asks, *"Why am I not in the Pro Bowl?"*

In my case, it was because I didn't deserve to be. I had more I needed to do to truly differentiate myself.

The awards would come. Fortunately for me, they didn't come so early that I was robbed of the teachings this experience was prepared to offer.

Once again, I only had to listen.

STRAIGHT TALK

Your ability to effectively use your mirror and your magnifying glass will go a long way in determining the success of your career climb. They will never be perfect optics on you or the world, but they can be transformative if we choose to make them tools that build greater acuity on what is real.

Find someone with a balance in the two and you have discovered an individual with an advanced Emotional Intelligence.

And genius level EQs are uncommon in the corporate world.

ADVERSITY AND RESILIENCE

"If there is no struggle, there is no progress."
~Frederick Douglass

My dad had a set of coiled springs that he used for exercising when I was a kid. They had wooden handles on each end and you could hold them at arm's length in front of you and then stretch them out until your arms were fully extended, pulling against the strength of the coils. You could add more springs depending on how strong you were. One was about my limit, but sometime around my early teen years I picked up a set one day and decided I was ready to move up. I added a second spring and promptly began to strain to complete a set. Somewhere around the sixth rep the handle in my left hand slipped from my grip and like a rubber band stretched too far, it came roaring back, smacking me solidly just below my eye—leaving one heck of a shiner. I was embarrassed. I was a chubby little 14-year-old and my dad wanted me to use the springs when he was around. Pop was always fit and he pulled those darn things easily. I never really exercised and couldn't be sure I ever would after that experience.

I lay the springs down and reached for some potato chips. Exercise, I decided, just wasn't my thing.

But it bugged me at some level. I started to look at those darn springs as something of a personal challenge—a piece of metal and wood that mocked me. After a few weeks (and after my eye had healed) I picked them back up and tried again.

And in the weeks that followed I added push-ups. Then my dad got me a set of cheap plastic weights from Sears and a chin-up bar. And over the course of one summer I lost 26 pounds of fat and developed a level of fitness that I could not have dreamed of attaining. More important, I started to replace unhealthy habits with better options and developed a lifestyle that was to stay with me the rest of my life. Forty years later I still work out with a passion that rivals that overweight young teenager. I can't be sure, but I believe those early lessons left an imprint on me that went much further than a push-up. I began to appreciate I could be what I wanted to be—I could reinvent myself—if I was willing to put in the work.

I've thought of those long lost springs occasionally over the years. I wish I had them on a wall somewhere. They taught me a lot more about life than I would have guessed possible.

They gave me a black eye and taught me how to see.

You'll get your share of corporate black eyes. I've never yet met anyone who has managed to glide through their career without problems or challenges; whose paths were always well lit and clear.

They don't exist out here in the real world, and the sooner you divorce yourself from this unrealistic vision the better off you will be.

Crucibles are the very real tests we will experience in our lives. And whether we want to appreciate it or not, everyone faces them.

But here is the secret many don't really grasp soon enough. They can become one of your greatest gifts.

Show me anyone who has survived multiple years in the corporate world and I will point you to someone who had to overcome burdens along the way.

There is an old saying that goes, *"It's not what happens to you in life but how you respond to it."*

The biggest difference I've seen in the real survivors in industry has been just that—how they chose to deal with adversity.

Some see a hurdle and they fret, worry, or turn away. Others see a hurdle and recognize a new challenge to overcome—an opportunity to develop new muscles and new skills. And just as you must tear down muscle via exercise in order for it to grow back stronger, the same applies to much of what we encounter in our careers.

A number of years back I took on what I considered to be a hugely challenging role with an eye on using the experience to springboard me into a higher position in the company. For 18 months I toiled in a very different job—always looking toward the anticipated "payoff" down the road.

Until the day came that I realized the *"promise"* some had suggested would follow my assignment was never going to happen. Instead I received a hearty *"thank you and job well done,"* and was promptly plugged back into a position similar to where I had been before.

For a time I was angry and even a little bitter; until it dawned on me I was falling victim to the same affliction that had fueled my first years with the company.

I call it Title Blindness, the overwhelming sickness that drives many to pursue the next rung on the ladder and forget that it is the experience of the climb that is what matters most. That interim role had offered me an incredible set of opportunities to learn more about my business. No one could take that away.

How we choose to approach problems goes a long way in how we overcome them. And the healthiest approach is to have the freedom of spirit that allows you to step back, accept them as a new chapter in your life, and challenge yourself to develop the skill sets to persevere.

Losing or making mistakes can paralyze us. But the real winners are the few who recognize there is no failure if we grow from the missteps. And we are talking about another of the core skill sets that distinguish survivors from those who are cast aside. Survivors don't dwell on their errors; they recognize they can use them to get better. They are willing to pay that price in order to continue their journey.

In the scientific arena there is a growing body of experts that point toward an interesting theory on the ascent of man, one that flies at least somewhat in the face of many other accepted models. It suggests that catastrophism has played a major role in our history and which peoples survived while others became extinct. Its thesis is simply this—history has seen periods of great disaster that virtually wiped out civilizations, only to see them reborn elsewhere. Those who flourished may have had less to do with natural selection or even greater knowledge and more to do with being in the right place at the right time—or maybe at the wrong place at the wrong time. Or perhaps the survivors may have been the best at managing to pick up the pieces after calamity and move on.

One thing is certain—hang around long enough in the corporate world and you will at some point encounter your own mini-version of catastrophe. I can count at least four different times in my career when I questioned if I would ever make it through.

Each of them turned out to be a 10-million-dollar experience I wouldn't give a dime to repeat. But I learned along the way and some of those lessons I carry with me. My **Adversity Formula** is pretty basic but you can bet it is battle-tested. Six basic steps when the dark clouds arise:

- Remain **calm**. In times of crisis you must look beyond the current circumstances and not allow the immediacy of your environment to dictate your outlook. The present storm will pass. You can make the decision you are tougher than the immediate stressors. People will either look to you for guidance or they will look away. I have never encountered true leaders who didn't understand the influence of their own emotions.

- **Constantly** assess your resources. Whether that's physical resources or other people, make certain you are clear on what you can bring to bear to address the current situation. Few crises are happening for the first time.

- **Leverage** the power of information to build a quality **plan.**

- Remain **confident** as you execute that plan. I sometimes asked myself how the very best leaders I had ever met would react in my situation, and I used that to persevere through some tough times. Maybe it was my own version of "fake it until you make it," but confidence is a powerful agent in overcoming adversity.

- **Measure** your progress—an amazing productivity tool. Even the most reluctant of employees rally when they see evidence that your plan is working.

- **Adjust/adapt** your plan accordingly.

Some of the most resilient people I've ever met have the unique capacity to look at life's obstacles in a very different way. They can't always overcome every pitfall but they almost always seek what can be gained from the experience—and they constantly look to reinvent themselves.

A good friend and former business colleague of mine wrote an incredible book about the crucibles of leadership and his personal journey. Jan Rutherford was an undersized young man (physically at least) with a big dream. Jan's book talks about how he overcame physical limitations to become a Green Beret, and then parlayed that into an extremely successful business and consulting career. For your suggested reading library, consider *The Littlest Green Beret; On Self-Reliant Leadership*. I often carry it with me as I travel. It reconfirms how the tests we face in our lives can truly be difference makers.

It was written by one of the biggest men I ever met.

STRAIGHT TALK

It's not always going to break your way. Be glad when it doesn't. Experience is over-rated. Adversity based experience isn't.

IT AIN'T FAIR
BUT IT'S THERE

"Do not take life too seriously.
You will never get out of it alive."
~Elbert Hubbard

There is no true meritocracy in the corporate world. Capitalism is a wonderful experiment but it is still a very imperfect one.

And if you hang around long enough you will come out with some bruises that will reinforce that fact. One of my managers early in my career was a natural humorist who always managed to find the irony in life. One of his favorite quotes as we debated quota methodologies or target assignment or other areas I could not get my head around was also the title of this chapter.

His message was more than a sardonic commentary on the business world. It challenged me to accept the fact that not everything was going to roll as I wanted. Confronting reality can be painstaking for many of us. Wishing it wasn't so might feel good, but it accomplishes nothing.

I've spent many hours as a leader in walking employees through the acceptance process—either around a policy they did not agree with or a company guideline they did not believe was fair or a decision they deemed inappropriate—and advancing from feelings to facts to solutions can be pretty difficult. And if the truth be told, sometimes walking myself through that process was just as challenging.

Somewhere in the world tonight an innocent person will be the victim of a terrible crime, a drunk who never should have been on the road will kill a driver, and a family will get the word that their beloved child has passed away.

It will not be fair.

So much of the challenge (for all of us) involves simply acknowledging the harsh reality—of reality.

We may not always like every company edict. Sometimes we may be able to change it or at least push back, but I will tell you that not every aspect of your career will always be fair.

And the counterbalance that it took me a long, long time to reconcile and put into context—the larger **Power of Gratitude**. At some point in my professional life I began to make it a point to take at least a few seconds each day to reflect on the blessings I enjoyed. Sometimes that tied back to my company. More often it tied back to my life—my family, my faith, my friends. Like so many struggling to *"fight the fight"* I was guilty of not always *"seeing the light."*

Here's what I learned: Five minutes of reflection on the things I was grateful for was more than a mind game. It drastically changed my outlook. And perspective, I was to learn, was a game changer.

STRAIGHT TALK

Your ability to look beyond your own provincial view of the world is critical in your development as a Corporate Survivor. Accept the imperfection, decide on what you can do that will make it better in the places you can influence, and move on.

My old boss was right.

PIVOTAL MOMENTS

"You don't get the same moment twice in life."
~Anonymous

History is fraught with examples of when the course of human events was forever altered by the actions of a few; individuals who were prepared to truly seize the moment in time when circumstances demanded greatness.

The same is true in the corporate world. In your career there may be long periods of the mundane, but trust me when I say there will be brief interludes where, if you're prepared to optimize them, you will shape your career in ways you may never imagine.

Potential career accelerators; potential career decelerators.

And unless you're intuitive enough to recognize them they will pass you by in the blink of a second and be lost.

Some of the best Corporate Survivors I've met are just like their counterparts on the playing fields of sports or the pages of history—they savor those chances to distinguish themselves.

And when their time comes, they deliver.

My first pivotal moment came early in my career when the powers-that-be would routinely descend on our National Sales School to assess talent, provide feedback to leadership, and scout prospects. My trip to that home office-based meeting was my first to a gathering of top performers from across the country, and I knew, as did everyone else, that only a part of these meetings were directed toward training. There was an equal part directed toward evaluation, determining who had the potential to be solid contributors in the short term. Our company was small, it was aggressive, and it did not have a high tolerance for average.

It turned out to be my first introduction to videotaped role-plays—sales calls that were filmed and then dissected for group discussion and for leadership review. I had no sales experience and recognized I would potentially be at a distinct disadvantage to others in our class who did. So I spent the better part of three evenings preparing for my time on camera, determined to actually demonstrate legitimate skills in my presentation versus the dumb luck example I offered in my initial interview (which I'll talk about later.) That meant investing a disproportionate amount of time reviewing clinical modules and our sales call model. That had a lot less to do with my eagerness to perform by the way. I just had no background and I knew a lot of the other participants did.

I got lucky because of the extra effort. My video was one that was selected as a guide for the class and ended up attracting the attention of some very important people in sales leadership.

It was a minor event in the course of normal company day-to-day, but for a guy with no history, no legacy, and no foundation—huge.

And it made me understand something early on that carried with me. Much of what I would do on a daily basis would likely go unnoticed, until it got very noticed. When those few key moments emerged that made a difference, I had to be prepared to distinguish myself.

Sometimes I was able to do that in the years that followed. Other times, not so much.

Now, here's the hard part for you, Corporate Survivor. Most of the time you don't recognize pivotal moments till they're past. No one will walk alongside you on the trail and whisper in your ear, *"Here it comes, get ready."* So you have to use a little bit of intuition and good judgment and watch the world around you.

Closely.

But if you can begin to understand that not every hour, not every day, not every week is created equally, you will begin to appreciate the importance of timing in your career. And like most of the rest of life, timing is everything.

A friend of mine once complained to me that he never got the lucky breaks he saw more successful corporate climbers enjoy. He was right. He was tone deaf to the world around him. When he was asked to deliver on a project, he responded with an average work product. When a corporate leader asked to work with him, he did no additional preparation to distinguish himself. When a major initiative demanded *"all hands on deck,"* he always made sure his contribution put him squarely in the middle of the pack.

No achiever ever began their day with a goal of someday hoping to become average.

STRAIGHT TALK

Average is below average in corporate. Get used to it. Anything that puts you in the middle of the bell curve assures you that someday the bell will ring on your career.

Corporate Survivors understand the magic of the Pivotal Moment, and when it comes—they deliver.

ANOTHER BRICK
IN THE WALL

*"People who think they know everything
are a great annoyance to those of us who do."*

~Isaac Asimov

You don't invest a career in corporate without appreciating a very predictive malady that afflicts most companies at some point.

The industry changes—companies falter. When hard times emerge it's not uncommon to see trusted peers whisked away, or to watch departments or divisions become a casualty of war. Anger around why things have changed bubbles to the surface. Whispers of doubt begin to creep into the water cooler conversation.

And construction on the wall begins in full.

The wall is the separator between "us and them"—the imaginary line of demarcation that allows us to defend our vision of what should be from the idiots who clearly are not as wise or as experienced as we are.

Cynicism and all of its manifestations are a normal part of the corporate world, and I suspect it is at least somewhat healthy. It allows us to engage in catharsis and vent for a while. It even restores a little control to our lives, and it can provide a remarkable repository to attach blame when we feel most compelled to point out the shortcomings of others. Remember the mirror and the magnifying glass chapter earlier? The wall is what arises when you have two totally broken tools at play, and their disrepair can do more than affect an individual—it can afflict entire companies.

It took me years to appreciate the phenomenon of the wall was not limited to one particular level of the company. Nor was it always bottoms up with employees lower in the organization casting aspersions on leadership. Sometimes it's just as apparent at the top and moves down through the company. Bottom line—no structure is impervious to the insidious influence of the wall.

Someone told me something once that always gives me perspective on its origins. *"Success,"* he offered, *"has a thousand fathers, but failure is and always will be an orphan. The only problem is no one wants to take the paternity test—it's a lot easier to point at more likely culprits."*

The wall is not impenetrable, but once erected it can compromise your individual effectiveness and your company's future—if you allow it.

Over the years I began to realize that no one in my company got up in the morning asking, *"How can I find a way to screw up everyone else's life today?"* Like you, they went about their business trying to make a positive difference.

Understanding that helped me make decisions around what I could do to help minimize, and in some cases, even help tear down the wall. They were simple changes but in time it helped me reduce my "victim's mentality" and begin to own a bit more personal accountability. They included:

> • Recognizing the danger of rumor and innuendo. Nothing kills speculation more effectively than the truth. Whenever possible I committed to dealing with facts—not assumptions.

> • I quit using "need to know" in my verbiage. I didn't work for the CIA—I worked for a health-care company. There was seldom information so secret that it couldn't be talked about openly.

> • I respected the difficulty others had in their roles, and challenged myself to step into their shoes and not just accept my view from the cheap seats.

> • I asked questions and sought to understand before I rushed to judgment.

> • I worked hard to create channels for input, idea sharing, best practices, and good old-fashioned dialogue. It helped me to appreciate that the wall was

almost the corporate equivalent of racism. We choose to look down or criticize others because we never come in contact with them. Communication that was honest and open made that much more difficult.

STRAIGHT TALK

It's easy to run a company when you're not the person doing it. And it's easy to sit at the top and point out others' failure to execute when you're not the one charged with that execution. Walls might be partially erected by companies but only individuals can make them strong.

You can redraw the lines that separate "us and them"—it is simply a matter of choice.

One brick at a time.

MEA CULPA

*"There is nothing noble in being superior to some other man.
The true nobility is being superior to your previous self."*

~W.L. Sheldon

Humility is not a widely celebrated character trait in much of the corporate world. Egos grow with success and few of us embrace the notion of putting our light under a basket. After all, there are a lot of Alphas out there—who wants to walk around with an overdose of modesty?

It took me a number of years to appreciate the dangerous effects of egotism and the corresponding power of humility. I watched highly talented employees repeatedly trip over their inflated sense of self-worth. And truth be told, I was not always willing to take my own tendencies into account—there were a lot of pats on the back and more than a few times I began to drink the Kool-Aid.

I can remember making a terrible hire early in my management career and struggling to deny my accountability for the employee's failure to perform—until I had no choice. It compromised my growth. The attempted cover-up hurt no one but me. Over time I began to appreciate assuming full accountability for my actions also meant demonstrating the ethical courage to admit when I was wrong—and actually table an often-overfed ego. That mirror we talked about earlier can distort our reflection. Mine sure has been on more than a few occasions.

When you're in the arena, it's not quite as easy to acknowledge mistakes as you might imagine. In fact, it's pretty darn tough.

Much of the world you are a part of now is highly competitive.

But developing the courage to own both the successes and the failures goes a long way in your growth as a Corporate Survivor—and even more in forming other's opinions of you.

Experience can be a wonderful teacher, but even the most gifted instructor in the world is rendered useless by the student incapable of learning. Egotism is often its greatest adversary.

I've worked with more than my share of tenured colleagues who boasted of their years in the industry and were repeatedly outperformed by comrades who had far less time. Twenty-five years of consecutive non-learning does not enhance your résumé. It simply makes you a candidate for the next downsizing.

And on the opposite extreme, the ones who maintained perspective never really read their individual press clippings, and truly owned every aspect of their job—including the courage to admit when they were wrong. In doing that they not only built on their foundation of trust and integrity but they also sent a message that said, *"We all make mistakes. How do we learn from them?"*

The inverse is equally true. Nothing breeds contempt quicker than a colleague who can never acknowledge error.

There may be no more lethal a self-inflicted wound than the sin of arrogance, and yet corporate can breed it quicker and more emphatically than perhaps any other medium.

I can remember sitting in a crowded meeting hall early in my career and watching as a highly placed senior leader (I'll call him Matthew for the purposes of the story) was introduced to the audience. A peer seated beside me leaned over and whispered, *"Get ready, Matthew is the smartest guy Matthew ever met."*

I never forgot that comment.

STRAIGHT TALK

We all have egos. No one sees us in as favorable a light as we see ourselves. The mirror is powerful if we are willing to look at it and ask the tough questions. It's even more powerful when we're willing to answer those questions.

BORIS

"If there is any one secret to success, it lies in the ability to get the other person's point of view and see things from that person's angle as well as your own."

~Henry Ford

Much to my disappointment, every day I learn that my view of the world may not be all-inclusive and quite as lucid as I believe it to be.

Neither is yours.

We have our own blind spots, myopia, and personal stigmatism, and each of them colors our world in ways we may not fully appreciate. Surviving the corporate world may require you to occasionally take steps to broaden that view.

Easy to say—tough to play.

I learned something about that broader view years ago and from an unlikely source. His name was Boris Spassky and if he sounds familiar it's because he's considered one of the greatest chess players in history—the archnemesis of American champion Bobby Fischer and a prodigy who's career spanned more than 50 years.

Spassky fascinated me because of an article I once read about how he worked the chessboard. He was active. He moved. He walked. He sometimes stepped away and then back. In the sometimes-staid world of chess, he was a jitterbug. Some assumed it was to disconcert his opponent, and that certainly might be the case, but Spassky asserted it was something more.

He claimed the broader perspective allowed him to more objectively assess his situation and more effectively understand the basis for his competitor's approach. In his own way, I think he recognized even five minutes in the other guy's shoes changed everything.

I believe Boris's lesson applies to much of life—especially corporate life. And it can get increasingly difficult the more experienced we get. But through much trial and error I have begun to appreciate the effort in better understanding a problem or issue from the viewpoint of the other person can be powerful—very powerful.

To do that you have to take the time to figuratively get up and move around the table and demonstrate the courage to look through the magnifying glass of the other person.

Most of us invest much time in building a strategy only from one perspective—our own. I know I sure have.

And the truly scary part—I've found my tendency to quickly draw opinions and conclusions only increases with time and experience.

Hey, I've seen just about everything in my career—and probably twice. That can (and has) occasionally created a recipe for disaster.

STRAIGHT TALK

You never stop learning. If you do, turn in your resignation. Try to challenge yourself to "walk around the table." You may stumble over your ego but those few steps are easier than you may think. Remember old Boris. A broader view can be a difference maker.

Checkmate.

PRESENT AND
ACCOUNTED FOR

"If you are depressed, you are living in the past.
If you are anxious, you are living in the future.
If you are at peace, you are living in the present."

~Laozi

Ever had to back your car down a long and winding road? Before the advent of today's bumper cameras, if you're like most, you had to resort to the old *"look over my right shoulder and hope"* approach, awkwardly guiding your vehicle while alternately shifting your attention from the back to the front to the back again.

If you happen to have a driveway that is anything other than a straightaway, you'll be able to gauge how many of your friends can actually back up. The tire tracks in your front yard are a dead give-away.

Much of your corporate journey could end up the same way, with you spending a lot of time looking over your shoulder—or worse yet—glancing in the rearview mirror while still trying to look forward.

Trying to figure out whether you should be looking forward or behind you is a dilemma that is very real.

You play the game long enough you will make mistakes, you will cultivate adversaries, and you will find you are something less than perfect. Good for you; you've engaged enough to give yourself an opportunity to grow.

How quickly you learn to regroup and move forward will be critical. Resiliency and perseverance are characteristics of true Corporate Survivors, and it's a skill that is essential for the long haul.

You're like the NFL kicker who misses a field goal or the PGA player who fails to sink the six-footer. Pick up and move on.

The other extreme can be just as compromising.

I'm a planner. Planners invest a lot of time looking into the future and figuring out how they will proactively address issues before they become issues. It's a habit that I developed over time and I don't apologize for.

But there is an admitted downside for inherent planners that warrants calling out. You spend too much time looking forward you will rob yourself of the importance of taking care of today.

What happened yesterday is a memory. What might happen in the future is a hope. What matters is what happens today—this moment—right now.

There's a robin that frequented our breakfast window the better part of one summer. It engaged in a pitched battle with its reflection, which offered more than its share of comic relief to our family—until it disintegrated into a sad study in frustration for the bird and mindless tapping for anyone in the back of the house.

I was reminded of that little bird as I considered some of the self-inflicted wounds we occasionally administer to ourselves in the daily course of events in the corporate world—at war with our own reflection.

There are a lot of achievers in the business world. And achievers sometimes pick battles with a competitor they can never beat—only beat down.

Themselves.

That tiny voice that offers us insight when we look in the mirror can sometimes mislead. It can drive us to the point of frustration when we fail to live up to a standard that may not always be attainable.

I remember a vacation I took with my family on the heels of a personnel decision that had demanded more time and effort than I intended. The issue had not been completely resolved as we departed, and for the better part of the next several days I did a rerun of what I should have done and how I could have reacted more quickly to the situation.

I was convinced I had made mistakes and faulted myself for not recognizing warning signs that would have brought us to resolution more effectively.

I was the robin.

And that damn mirror wasn't going anywhere until I managed to put it away.

STRAIGHT TALK

The ability to live purposefully—to focus on the present—
is a challenge. Our natural tendency is often to dwell on
past successes (or failures) or fixate on the uncertainty of
the future. But the only thing we can fully influence is this
moment. Allowing the shadows of the past or the imaginings
of the future to compromise the precious present is a malady
that impacts all of us from time to time.

Sometimes the best course of action is remarkably simple.

Fly away.

PART TWO
THE KEY CHAIN

THE KEY CHAIN

"When we are no longer able to change a situation,
we are challenged to change ourselves."
~Viktor Frankl

It took me the better part of two decades to finally embrace the critical importance of the three Keys discussed in the chapters to follow. The practical examples offered represent hard-earned lessons.

Survival begins with the Compass. Thriving is another matter. Embrace the Keys and your future will become infinitely clearer.

> • **Leadership** is the distinguishing characteristic of great companies. It permeates and becomes a part of the culture. And the very best create a pipeline for the generations to come. Your ability to lead, regardless of the level you enjoy in your company, will either accelerate or derail your career. I'll offer practical advice on how you can pursue the former. We'll discuss the *"what"* and the *"how"* in very clear terms. Again, years of perspective condensed into a few simple chapters you can apply today.

> • **Communication** is the wind that drives your ship forward. I began my journey believing that

communication generally involved oratorical skills. In time I began to appreciate that the very best communicators relied far more on other aptitudes— aptitudes that the vast majority of the corporate world remained oblivious to. Consider the chapters on communication to be the insights gained. They changed my career trajectory dramatically.

• **Learning** was to become the supplemental resource that carried me beyond survival to truly thriving. Over time I realized it made my reliance on my company far less important. The human mind is like a muscle—if you challenge it, it will respond. If you allow it to grow stale it will atrophy. The decision to expand your skills by becoming a student of life is yours to make. My dad has a saying I've often reminded myself of when I think of corporate: *"If you let down you slow down, if you sit down you go down, and if you lay down you die."*

STRAIGHT TALK

Very few will enjoy the advantages the cardinal points of The Compass will offer their careers. And so they will embark on a series of trails that reach dead ends...or cliffs. For those that embrace its principles there is a path.

But finding a path is only the beginning. The Master Course follows in the chapters to come. Three skill sets that can differentiate you - and accelerate your journey IF you commit to understanding them.

LEADERSHIP

*"An army of sheep led by a lion can defeat
an army of lions led by a sheep."*
~African Proverb

Accept this simple premise as indisputable.

Your long-term career success is dependent on your ability to lead.

Divorce yourself from the assumption that if you don't have an interest in management in the formal sense then there is no benefit in better understanding the Keys behind effective leadership.

If that were the case, your best bet would be to open a hotdog stand on the corner. But unfortunately the most successful street vendor has to be able to influence others or he will go bust.

Here are a few of the practical insights my experience taught me over the years.

LEAD, FOLLOW, OR GET THE HELL OUT OF THE WAY

"A boss says Go! A leader says Let's go."

~E. M. Kelly

A former colleague and good friend taught me a valuable lesson about leadership a number of years ago that I often reflect on even today.

A small group of senior sales leaders were involved in a mini-meltdown in the last minutes before a major national meeting. I was relatively new to my latest leadership position, and my two senior colleagues were fumbling trying to finalize logistics before the curtain opened for our most important gathering of the sales organization for that year. The one assigned to lead the project was not particularly organized, struggled to get his mind around logistics, and was basically stumbling through the backstage prep while several thousand sales reps were assembling out front.

The clock was ticking and we were sinking into a self-induced quagmire that threatened our meeting. I watched senior colleague number two quietly listen, offer suggestions, and then grow more frustrated as the assigned point person rambled on.

At about five minutes before we were to go live, number two finally slammed his hand on the desk and said to his somewhat inept colleague, *"Look! Either lead, follow, or get the hell out of the way!"*

It was a surprising declaration from a man who always practiced diplomacy, but he recognized—as did all of us—that in the last seconds before we *"went live"* someone had to take charge. He did—and effectively.

Senior colleague number two took control of the situation, made a few last minute decisions, and then ensured an understanding of all assignments.

The meeting was saved. A five-minute period of time—but I never forgot the lessons learned.

STRAIGHT TALK

When critical events demand it, someone has to lead. Groups don't just automatically walk in the same direction through telepathic communication. Sometimes it requires courage to step into the void and to say to peers, *"Follow me."*

THE POWER TO INSPIRE

"I alone cannot change the world, but I can cast a stone across the waters to create many ripples."

~Mother Teresa

I still remember with amazing clarity my first weeks at what we called Initial Headquarter Training—a gathering of new people from around the country who went through an intensive three-week introduction on product knowledge, industry, and basic selling skills. High competition. High pressure. Several did not make it to completion. We were ranked, assessed, and evaluated from the time we arrived to the time we flew back to our respective home cities.

At the beginning of our third week there was a rustling one afternoon from the back of the classroom. I watched the instructor's face grow pale, followed the lead of every other student, and turned to see an older man standing there in a brilliant blue sports coat. There was a murmuring that told me this was not a typical guest. Our company's founder had decided to drop by unannounced.

Our teacher invited him to address the group with a reverence that might be demonstrated by a local priest if the pope had stopped by for a surprise communion. We watched him stride confidently to the front of the room.

It was my first interaction with a multi-millionaire, and his appearance could not have had a more stunning impact on most of us had he emerged from a spaceship in the middle of the company cafeteria. The legend of the man formed the very fabric of our company; a former salesperson himself, the stories of his rise from detail rep to founder of this company read like a mid-western version of a Damon Runyon novel.

We watched this larger-than-life figure as he approached the podium where he gazed out over the audience of 20-something-year-olds and said nothing—only fixing each of us with a steely gaze as if he were silently memorizing our names.

When he finally spoke he began with this: *"Well...you must be good or you wouldn't be here."*

I have never forgotten those words or the tone he set for this group of greenhorns.

The message was simple.

"I believe in you."

In time some of us began to believe in ourselves.

Two years later, I was tapped along with another 40 sales reps from around the country to be a member of an advance team for a new drug the company was releasing. This small group was to establish a beachhead with calls to specialists who were dotted across major cities—the premise being that a pyramid approach to a new brand would ensure greater adherence by primary care doctors later.

It was a backbreaking assignment with constant travel for a six-week period. Those of us selected were honored by the request and worn out by the commitment it required. But we knew how important this was to our company's future.

Four weeks into the project I got a phone call early on a Saturday morning that reinforced for me the impact of a leader.

I was still asleep when the call came and I remember my wife's excited voice as she tried to rouse me from my fatigue-induced slumber.

"It's Mr. K!" she yelled. *"He's calling from Kansas City and he wants to talk to you!"*

I seriously doubted our founder would be calling me and I protested as she shoved the phone into my hand.

And then I heard the voice and I snapped to attention.

"Tim, I just wanted to call you this morning and say thanks. How's it going out there?"

I stuttered through a barely coherent response and for the next five minutes this mega-rich entrepreneur and I talked about my adventures of the previous month. I can't say I remember what I said that day. But I will never forget the impression it made on me.

One man's call to a follower that said, *"What you're doing is important and I want you to know it's appreciated,"* reinvigorated me in ways I could not ever completely describe. His message was simple—I understand how tough this is. I need you to keep doing it.

This was the first leader I met who genuinely saw a future greater than I could imagine. And he helped me believe I could be a part of building it.

"You must be good or you wouldn't be here."

STRAIGHT TALK

If you're lucky you will encounter at least a few transformational leaders over the course of your career. Regardless of the many books that profess their commonality, they are not on every corner. Study them—learn from them—emulate them. They are the ones who enjoy the sweeping power to galvanize and inspire.

PUT ME IN COACH

*"I've learned that people will forget what you said,
people will forget what you did, but people will never forget
how you made them feel."*

~Maya Angelou

I used to play Monday night doubles tennis with a group of guys. It was pretty much an opportunity to compete, laugh, and drink a beer after work. We rotated who brought the cooler and spent the last hour of each evening swapping stories and offering our views on the world in general.

One of the four was a former Division One basketball player, a pretty good athlete who played at my alma mater—the University of North Carolina. His coach was the legendary Dean Smith.

I never met Coach Smith but like every self-respecting UNC grad I bow slightly at the mention of his name. Most legitimate basketball fans do the same. His legacy needs no elaboration from me.

But I saw one Monday night the impact of his reach—and I never forgot it.

My buddy the basketball player announced halfway through his first beer that he was cutting out early that night. He had work to do and calls to make that began early the next morning.

We waited for the punch line, and when there wasn't one he explained that he had received a phone call that day from Coach Smith. It's important to explain that this courtside conversation was around 2005, approximately 30 years since my very middle-aged colleague had worn the powder blue jersey of the UNC basketball team. Like the rest of the 50-something's gathered courtside, he was immersed very much in matters of career.

"Coach Smith calls me from time to time," my friend explained, *"and he asked me for some help."* He went on to say that a former UNC basketball player was moving to our Charlotte area and was, in Coach Smith's words, *"between jobs."* The old coach thought maybe my friend could help him with some introductions and open some doors.

"Got to get started early, I would like to give Coach Smith an update by early tomorrow afternoon," he continued.

The rest of us stared back at him with a bemused look.

Our friend explained, *"He called me. Coach Smith expects me to help him find a job."* He paused and then said, *"I can't let Coach Smith down."*

He was very serious. It was like he was 19 years old again and his coach was asking him to run wind sprints. And we knew that—come hell or high water—he was going to find that basketball player a job.

The rest of us learned something that night. The power of expectation—especially when the expectations come from someone who is highly respected—can be incredible. It can transform a middle-aged business executive into a teenage *"walk-on."*

Our friend added something that had equal effect on me. He said, *"Nothing would be more difficult for me than to know I let Coach Smith down. He believes I can move the world."*

I wondered how many times the words of a trusted mentor had created a similar effect on me. I already knew the answer. There have been times in my life when I knew someone so believed in me that I had no choice but to excel.

STRAIGHT TALK

If your life was ending tonight and you could go back through the years and enjoy a quiet final five minutes with the few people who changed you in a highly positive way, who would you reserve your time with? Remember their names—they were likely transformational leaders.

You've encountered thousands of people, but only a few made a profound difference. Much of our world is quid pro quo—transactional. We do what we do because we're rewarded for it.

Transactional interactions affect our hands and feet.

Transformative interactions affect our heart and head.

And they are timeless.

FIFTH FLOOR PLEASE

"The quality of a leader is reflected in the standards they set for themselves."

~Ray Kroc

I can remember the very moment—where I was and what I was doing—when I first believed I had a sustainable future with the company I had stumbled into.

A few years into my sales career I was tapped to enter our Leadership Development Program (LDP). The LDP was an accelerated training vehicle for employees who had been identified as having leadership potential. Given the expansion our company was getting ready to begin—a necessary step. We were about to grow from approximately 100 million to almost a billion in sales by the end of the decade.

My selection was a tremendous honor. I was young and green but I knew the chance to participate would potentially stamp me for greater responsibilities down the line. It came on the heels of my participation in what we called a Talent Development Center—two-plus days of intensive individual and group exercises that were used to assess your mental agility and capacity to lead. If you passed you got an invitation to the LDP.

I joined some 30 other employees in the training. Opportunities were emerging and the next wave of potential management candidates were about to be tested, compared, and potentially groomed for new roles. The stakes had suddenly grown higher.

Several weeks into the experience I attended a national sales meeting near our headquarters. A few hundred people assembled at a hotel there to learn more about our new brand strategies and to prepare for the changes to come.

On the second day I crowded into an elevator on the mezzanine level to make my way back to my room after a long round of meetings. I remember gazing blankly over a sea of mostly unfamiliar faces and then hearing someone from the other side say hello and call me by name.

The head of our Leadership Development Program smiled back at me and we exchanged a few pleasantries before the door to the fifth floor opened and he excused himself. It's important to note that I had opted to pass on my fourth-floor exit. I was pretty surprised he even knew who I was. With the exception of an exercise he had overseen in the development center, I couldn't remember even a brief conversation with him.

I rode the elevator back down and when I got to my room, called my wife and excitedly described my elevator encounter. It sounds a little maudlin now but to a young upstart trying to make a name, so very important. The single most important figure in our talent development program recognized me.

And at that moment I started to think about this place becoming a career.

It reconfirmed again how even the tiniest affirmation at the right time from the right person can make a difference.

It is amazing how often I failed to honor that in my interactions with others, forgetting that people who feel noticed and appreciated are capable of so much more.

As regards that senior leader and our brief elevator conversation, I was to learn his focus on people transcended brief sidebar conversations. He was to become the single most influential mentor for me in the company and I would end up working with him on several occasions over the 20 years to come.

He made it a point to seek out future leaders and cultivate relationships with them. And without ever consciously realizing it, he taught me that becoming a person of influence begins with building trust. In the intervening years I would watch his brand of professionalism make a mark on the entire company, and help to transform a sometimes *"good old boy"* culture into one that mirrored a higher set of values.

He was an incredibly demanding leader. But early on I began to appreciate he believed in me. And therein was a lesson I was to embrace. Highly valued leaders can demand so much more than others.

I still carry with me the simple phrase he would always make certain to offer as we fought together to build our business, sometimes in the midst of much turmoil.

"Tim, you're efforts are appreciated."

Five simple words but they came from someone whose opinion mattered. Like my tennis buddy and Dean Smith, the thought of letting him down sometimes haunted me. He expected me to be willing to take the big shot.

More important, he believed I could make it.

STRAIGHT TALK

The larger truth in the corporate world—all of us look for mentors. We seek them out long before we begin to try and interpret the mission of our department or company. Whether peer or supervisor, they are the differentiator for companies.

There is no more important dimension to an organization's success than leadership. Systems, strategies, products, and plans are all crucial, but without leadership, all the other components are destined to fail.

John Maxwell, in his book The 21 Irrefutable Laws of Leadership, speaks eloquently to what ultimately determines why employees buy into a vision, a strategy, or a company.

It begins with whether they buy into their leader.

WHY BEING EFFICIENT ISN'T ENOUGH

*"Sometimes it is not enough to do our best;
we must do what is required."*

~Winston Churchill

Most of the more competent managers have one common trait. They do things right. They are organized and they place a premium on order, organization, and systems. They are, in a word, efficient.

But there is a distinction between managers and leaders. Most, but not all leaders, are reasonably competent as regards the above skills. They enjoy some level of efficiency. But this is where they differ—competent leaders don't just do things right, they do the right things.

That's the difference in efficiency and effectiveness. One focuses on doing things right—the other focuses on doing the right things. One is primarily transactional, while the other can be transformational.

That quote at the beginning of this chapter from Winston Churchill, one of history's greatest leaders, resonates even today. In the crisis that was World War II, it was Churchill's voice that became the battle cry for Great Britain—one so resolute that a nation was compelled to follow.

Churchill, the leader, came at a time perfectly suited to the times. Ironically, as the war ground to a halt, his countrymen voted him out of office, sending him into premature retirement. Some historians surmise that his greatest leadership strengths were of less importance as peace came within reach.

Churchill, the manager, was suddenly very replaceable.

There are a great many people in the corporate world who do things right—but nothing happens. You will be hard-pressed to find people who do the right things and don't affect movement.

I learned that lesson when I was asked to join a group of senior leaders to conduct concurrence interviews for candidates as part of a national blitz to scale up one of our sales forces. Over the course of a two-day period, I joined each of these leaders and could watch firsthand their approach, their questions, and their overall interview style.

Senior Leader 1 was polished, exacting, well planned, and very organized. His interviews were, at least in my mind at the time, textbook.

Senior Leader 2 was far less polished, more than a little unorthodox, and had a style that would never make it into any book on candidate selection.

Senior Leader 1 did everything right and did not land on any quality decisions on new sales reps. I was to learn later that his track record was decidedly average when it came to bringing in new talent.

Senior Leader 2 not only identified and brought on board several outstanding associates, he also pinpointed several problem contenders that we effectively removed from the process.

I was astounded, and even more so when I learned the legacy of Senior Leader 2 was almost legendary. This was a longtime district manager who simply knew how to identify talent. But in my mind, his approach did not marry with any of the classroom instruction I had ever been exposed to.

It turned out to be a valuable lesson. You can be rock solid in doing things right and never really realize full potential. Senior Leader 2 understood what was most important in finding superstars. His approach was unconventional but he knew how to do the *"right things,"* a lesson I've carried with me a long time.

STRAIGHT TALK

Good managers do things right. And in times of stability they can be invaluable to a company—or to a nation. Whether it is in the personal management of their career or in guiding other people, it is a *"must have"* in the corporate world. Inefficiency usually dictates how far you will NOT go as regards cardinal point number one on the Compass—personal accountability.

Good leaders do the right things. And in times of true crisis, they are critical. Expecting to manage a company through crisis is akin to trying to manage an army into battle. History is replete with peacetime managers who failed in times of peril. The same holds true for you personally— you can manage your career when things remain status quo, but you'll need leadership agility to survive the times of turbulence.

Great leaders do the right things right. The pages of history are dotted with the few who truly transcended the role. So are the chapters of any successful company. The names may not be as familiar or their triumphs as noteworthy but they are there.

THE MEETING ROOM TEST

"Experience is the teacher of all things."

~Julius Caesar

Early in my career I began to study leaders and their influence, and ask myself questions around what made them respected and what engendered trust from others. It took me several years to appreciate that titles oftentimes had very little to do with true leadership. In fact, in some cases it wasn't the formal supervisor who enjoyed real influence.

One of the best venues I found to study the paradox of leadership—those meetings I referenced earlier. I started focusing on more than content. I began to watch the group, their interactions, and how they did or did not arrive at decisions.

And like card sharks that study the table and their competitors, I discovered *"tells"* that offered insights I've carried with me for a long time.

The meeting notes I collected evolved into other areas, and oftentimes taught me much more than the business agenda offered. Here are just a few of the other areas I learned to watch closely:

> • The leader eye contact. Even the most polished presenters will often sweep the room as they speak and then rest their attention on the individual whose opinion matters most—the participant of greatest influence. That conveys a very powerful message to the observer

of group dynamics: *"Everyone is important but it is your support that is most important to me."*

• Referral power—citing the expert. When an audience member wants credibility they align with the perceived *"alpha"* in the room to cement their point of view. That person of influence becomes the informal proof source. It signals to the rest of the group that your views are aligned. In other words, if you respect the alpha you should respect this contribution.

• Seating. Informal leaders generally will be placed in positions where they can establish eye contact easily with the formal meeting owner—seldom side by side. Smart meeting facilitators want the influencers where they can reach out to them easily.

• The meeting breaks—pivotal moments that many simply ignore. But take a close look at what happens when the formal sessions stop and participants can migrate on their own free will. Watch where the circles form.

• Question- or insight-driven meeting facilitation. Who asks the questions that provoke thought? Who asks the questions that evoke movement? I once watched a leader who had no formal role to play in a meeting ask two questions that not only redirected the flow but cast it in a direction that greatly changed the output. Two questions. And at the end the group was convinced their conclusions were ones they arrived at by themselves. Classic example of a leader operating at an optimal level. They did not dictate the outcome. Instead, they asked the question that provoked thought that led to the outcome. Powerful.

• Body language. Powerful *"physical listeners"* can enjoy a tremendous influence on a meeting. By physical I mean those who demonstrate active listening skills. They lean forward when others talk, they maintain diligent eye contact, and they check back to make sure they are clear on other's inputs. The inverse is equally true. Watch the less engaged who stare blindly ahead when others speak or—even more damaging—content themselves with their phone or laptop. Those who stay in the moment during meetings are infinitely more effective meeting contributors. Here's a suggestion that will help you gauge this even more. Watch closely in your next company gathering. Don't be surprised if when the participant of greatest influence laughs, you hear others follow suit. If they take notes other participants do the same. Even to the point of taking a drink of water. The term for that behavior—physical mirroring. But why can these simple observations be so very revealing? The answer is simple but timeless— people are hardwired to seek out leaders. The path isn't always clear. We naturally look toward those who confidently are striding the same trail as our own.

STRAIGHT TALK

Every group interaction can be a developmental laboratory if we choose to make it one more vehicle to build our career. Again, experience is not defined as accumulated years of existence—it's the accumulated years of learning.

R . E . S . P . E . C . T .

"I acknowledge no man as my superior, except for his own worth, or as my inferior, except for his own demerit."

~Theodore Roosevelt

I'll never forget the business review and presentation I was called to conduct with a panel of senior corporate heads—several weeks of preparation from multiple parties that led to one four-hour meeting.

And watching one member of the home office team who asked three or four perfunctory questions and then dived into his I Phone where he impatiently poured through his email messages until he chose to pull his head back up and offer some bit of "profound insight."

I might have been disappointed had I not seen that pattern of behavior repeat itself repeatedly over the next several years. The effect was devastating for the people who had worked so hard to prepare. The message was clear from the senior executive: *"I'm a busy person and what you have to say is not nearly as important to me as my latest email message."*

That leader had no idea he was eroding his relationship with potential followers. He had allowed his need to stay abreast of everything take the place of staying on top of the one thing that was most important.

But there was a more damaging effect. Respect is never simply accorded by title. It can only be earned by actions. And those actions would never be able to be recalled.

One of the easiest ways to damage respect is to make multi-tasking a priority over solo-tasking, particularly when the latter involves the people you work with—making what's most important most important.

The subject of respect goes a long way in the corporate world. There are a lot of behaviors that will build it with your colleagues, direct reports, or others, and a few that will damage it. A few examples to consider:

- Eye contact and staying in the moment. The best make you the center of their attention when they talk with you. I'll never forget the senior leader who was the absolute master, nor the one who would allow his eyes to dart across the room after the first minute of dialogue and begin to interject "uh huhs" when it was time to wrap it up and move along. The message was clear: "I have more important things to do."

- Listening. Not surface acknowledgement but true second-level listening. Not just content but the meaning behind the words. Most know when they are being patronized. And they don't forget.

- Onstage Oscar winners and offstage trolls. You stick around long enough in corporate and you will meet them; charismatic and motivating when "they're on" and withdrawn and reclusive when "they're off." If you depend on the lights to be an influencer in your organization, then you're better suited to Broadway.

- Condescension. Have experienced it very few times in my years in the corporate world and I never forgot it when I did. You may be more experienced, more skilled, or more powerful in your corporate hierarchy than the person you're working with, but there is never an excuse to not treat a counterpart with respect and dignity.

STRAIGHT TALK

What goes around comes around in the corporate world. None have more of a reciprocal impact than the behaviors that either build or erode respect.

THE FIVE

"If your actions inspire others to dream more, learn more, do more, and become more, you are a leader."

~John Quincy Adams

Suppose that tomorrow you were selected to be the new head of your department. The decision came down quickly and without warning. Yesterday you were one of the many. Today—well, today you get the chance to run things.

Your phone rings. Looks like a department meeting is already on the books.

Then the first gnawing pang of doubt begins to creep in. Your predecessor was less than beloved and you're glad she's gone. But what makes you think people will look at you any differently? In fact, who's to say they won't hate the fact you now have greater responsibilities—ones that some of them were in contention for.

Welcome to the Promotional Twilight Zone (PTZ)—that place where your dreams and ambitions come face-to-face with the *"reality of now."* You've worked awfully hard to get to this uncomfortable place.

The PTZ is a flashback to the same feelings you had when you started your corporate journey—new role, uncertainty, and fear—in other words, new terrain. Remember the trail's head when you stumbled along trying to find a path?

But with experience comes learning—sometimes.

If you have navigated even a year in the corporate world you've begun to appreciate there is something that distinguishes leaders (regardless of title) from a great many others. And there is an intangible people look for when they seek out the few they are willing to partner with—or follow. Basic questions they need answers to in order to justify their faith.

Learn these universal questions and you are halfway there as regards becoming a leader—but only halfway. They speak easy but play hard. Because the answers are not in the words you speak but in the actions you take.

I call them **The Five**. Commit them to memory and do not doubt that every meaningful relationship in your life in someway tied back to how you answered these questions—or didn't. Your best friend had them when they first met you, your spouse had them when he or she began to consider you as a lifelong partner, and you can darn well bet any co-worker you will ever meet has them too.

The questions apply equally to how we look at others. The next time you vote for a political candidate, look at a supervisor, consider the salesperson you might choose to buy from, or sit on the examining table and listen to your physician wax on about your health care—consider The Five. They're an internal radar system we all carry but may not fully activate.

You have two challenges when it comes to leadership. First, understand **The Five** and their importance. Second, decide how prepared you are to answer them in your interactions with others.

The Five:

> • **Are you credible?** Few blindly follow, or even listen to those they don't believe warrant their attention. Forget your title or the product you're pitching. People don't follow titles—they follow people. Over the years I came to appreciate two factors that dictated my assessment of credibility. Each was remarkably simple:
>
>> • The first—authenticity. Those few who were real—not manufactured or adorned in *"corporate speak"*—were often easy to spot. Posers seldom *"walked the talk."* I learned quickly to match words with actions.
>>
>> • The second—competency. We don't willingly partner with anyone we believe is not capable. I

saw numerous situations throughout my career of individuals fighting out of their weight class. Capability is a core requirement. It can't be faked—at least not for long.

• **Do you care about me?** No employee will willingly follow a leader whose only interest is in driving business. No players line up behind a coach they don't see as legitimately interested in them. Oh, they may comply but they will never fully commit. In your own life think about the individuals who you believed were credible and truly cared about you. That fifth-grade teacher who influenced your love of music, the mentor who offered you lessons you carry even today, your mom's comforting voice when you believed college admissions was going to end your life.

• **Can I trust you?** The very best leaders are people of integrity who, even if you don't agree with them, you know can be trusted to act fairly and honestly. The greatest test of loyalty is in earning trust. Trust is nothing more than a reciprocal agreement to believe.

Civil War Confederate general Robert E. Lee was a legendary leader—the level of respect from both comrades and adversaries almost godlike. Belief in their leader sustained a beaten Confederate army long past what should have been their termination date. Lee never forgot his obligation to his troops and suffered much personal guilt over the terrible toll his men suffered in the final days of the war. A few years after the surrender at Appomattox, Lee made his way back to a reunion with his comrades at the storied Greenbrier Hotel in White Sulfur Springs, West Virginia. The story goes that Lee was troubled about attending. He had never returned for similar functions, fearful perhaps that he could not look into the eyes of those he felt he had failed. But as he entered the Grand Ballroom on that fateful day the roar of gratitude from the men overwhelmed him. The accounts of newspapers at that time recount the reverence that swept the floor as this legendary man came into view, each successive wave of veterans rising in a crescendo that shook the chandeliers. The general they affectionately called "The Old Man" had come back to them. And every follower in that room was moved to tears, every bit as respectful as before.

Trust is a powerful driver. Earn it and a lot of other inadequacies can be forgiven.

• **Are you committed to a vision of excellence?** Key words—commitment, vision, and excellence. Not just profitability or the latest quarterly earnings report—true excellence. Do you have a vision for the future that others can buy into, and does it align with their values and principles? Does your commitment ensure you are prepared to act to ultimately realize that vision? Are you prepared to walk the talk? Commitment cannot be faked—at least not for long. But it's only when it's matched with a grander vision for the future that others truly align.

• **Can you help make me (or my situation) better?** Each of the above questions matter little if you can't help others realize their goals—improve their station. The people you associate with are the people who make you better. The leaders you follow are those who optimize your potential. The salespeople you buy from are those who improve your life.

STRAIGHT TALK

The Five separate individuals of influence from the masses. They are universal tenets and their applicability extends to your personal relationships as well. Put them to the test when you consider the people who have been most important in your life.

Over my years of service, the few truly transformational leaders I encountered in someway intuitively understood the concepts on which The Five are based, whether they codified them as I have here or not. If you're serious about optimizing your leadership capabilities, use them as your litmus test to gauge yourself. At some level I suspect most of us recognize their importance. The question: Are we prepared to make certain our actions will answer them?

STAR LIGHT, STAR BRIGHT

"Justice is like the North Star, which is fixed, and all the rest revolve around it."

~Confucius

Constant, unwavering, and trustworthy—real leaders are vital in times of normalcy, but they become essential in times of crisis.

The very best recognize others will listen to their words but watch their feet. If they're worried and unsure, you can bet followers will be terrified. If they're cynical, others become mutinous. If they have doubts, others become true nonbelievers.

Over my career I began to appreciate that in moments of turmoil leaders become irreplaceable. Just as an army learns in times of battle where the true commanders are, so it is for the corporate world in periods of crisis.

I saw that through the wave of downsizings. Empathetic leaders soared. Bottom-line managers simply endured.

I can remember one who single-handedly rallied a very demoralized team around him because his faith and belief in the future helped others to survive. He reached out to peers, he checked on them, and yes - he pulled them along through his own strength of spirit.

And I realized leaders didn't require the conferral of titles. In fact, some of the very best held no supervisory responsibilities. But they were credible. They cared. They were trusted. And they had a vision for what could be.

I also saw the opposite effect. I once watched a leader who had built a legacy of success abandon those values in a moment of crisis and collapse into a period of total self-absorption. Those around him watched their leader effectively turn his back on followers. They floundered. Many left. But the greatest disappointment was in watching the sudden loss of respect for someone who had worked so long to build it.

It taught me that truly effective leaders always manage to make sure they put first the people who execute and who make strategy come to life. The others focus more on execution and people often become an afterthought.

It also reminded me of tough feedback I had received when I first went through our company's Management Development Center, a multi-day assessment process to identify potential future leaders. That program was the ultimate *"pass-fail"* for those who wanted to advance their careers. You got a green light—your career moved to the next level. Red light meant *" get content with where you are because you aren't going to be doing anything else for a while."*

One of my feedbacks hit close to home. In essence it was this: *"Just because you may know what you believe are the right answers is no guarantee others will follow you. Your ability to build real followership will be dependent on helping others, not just coming up with solutions."*

Translation—you're not quite as smart as you may think you are. And even if you're right it won't make any difference if no one else is inclined to follow you. Leadership, Mr. Cole, is not a check-the-box exercise.

Over the years I finally came to appreciate this simple point.

STRAIGHT TALK

You cannot be a person of influence if you don't take the time to listen to those around you, to appreciate their viewpoints, to tap into their strengths, and to demonstrate true empathy for what is important to them. Your foundation is built on credibility and not on what you think you know.

Your challenge is not always going to be in providing answers. More often than not, it will be in asking the right questions. The very best help others to look at their own mirror.

WHY, TELL ME WHY

"There are two great days in a person's life—the day we are born and the day we discover why."

~Unknown

In one of my early roles I worked for an individual who decided he would be intimately involved in every aspect of his direct reports' lives, to a sometimes nauseating degree. Every metric known to man was scrutinized, debated, and reanalyzed. The atmosphere was tense and the degree of local ownership was nonexistent.

How could there be ownership when the only real owner was the boss? The direct reports were merely pawns in the grand scheme and made to feel more like victims. They were left to worry from week to week if they hit the mark on the latest grid. More important—they lost sight of their primary purpose and the real customer.

In fact it could be said the manager became the primary customer. And so total focus shifted there as well.

It was my first introduction to a Mike—my tag for a micromanager. I would see Mike again over the course of my years of service—of course, with a different name and a different face, but it was the same person. Mikes don't just disappear. They are in every company and they can and sometimes do serve a useful purpose.

But they will not build sustainable greatness.

Over time I began to realize there is a spectrum involved in leading and managing other people. Think of it as advancing from absolute autocracy to some form of enlightened egalitarianism—from monarch to consensus builder. It was only when I had worked with all types of people in leadership roles that I began to appreciate how truly different and effective the various approaches could be.

And I finally reconciled a fact I've carried with me for a very long time:

> Those who cannot lead…will, at best, hope to manage.
>
> Those who cannot manage…will, at best, hope to control.
>
> Those who cannot control…will, at best, hope to coerce.

Not surprisingly, you'll find the Mikes on the control and coercion side of the spectrum.

I've worked with thousands of people in the course of my career and a majority were competent in handling things, in overseeing what needed to be done. It was business guru Peter Drucker who first described management as involving five basic components: controlling, planning, staffing, directing, and organizing. Though much has changed in industry, these pieces remain as critical today as when Drucker first coined them over a half century ago.

All of us are compelled to in some way manage. It's pretty difficult to navigate a career without basic management skills. Our colleges effectively turn out highly prepared succeeding generations who understand the underpinnings of business, and many go on to be qualified people managers at some point in their careers. Much of management is transactional—do the things I say and I will reward you.

But leadership is another matter. I believe at least some of its curriculum can only be accessed on the battlefield.

History offers us a remarkable example.

In 1933, newly elected President Franklin Roosevelt had to deal with a general public so frightened by the economic collapse that they stormed the banks demanding their money, and oftentimes resorting to burying their hard-earned dollars in their backyards or stuffing their money underneath their mattresses for protection.

Our nation stood on the brink of true financial ruin and our leader faced a challenge that today is difficult to even begin to comprehend. Faith in our monetary system was failing, replaced by panic and uncertainty. There was legitimate fear that American capitalism was on its last legs.

Roosevelt made the decision to go directly to Americans, and the first of the fireside chats was born. In that first 15-minute *"talk"* he explained to people huddled around their radios the basics of our banking system, why it had failed, and the steps our government would do to correct it moving forward. More important, he asked our countrymen to have faith that money deposited in local banks would not only help restore our economy but was essential to beginning the long climb to economic recovery.

Many historians suggest that single speech turned the tide for our country. The next day, citizens buoyed by the confidence of their president, began to bring their money back to their banks. Many were the very same who days before had marched in the streets demanding a full accounting of their funds.

Roosevelt did not demand compliance. He did not coerce Americans. He did not dictate what had to be done. He spoke to his countrymen on a human level. He began to gain their trust and he helped them understand that simply maintaining the status quo—of doing nothing at all—would be disastrous.

He demonstrated a simple but incredibly powerful approach that transformational leaders always intuitively seem to understand.

Inspiring others begins first with addressing the why—not the what.

It took me a long time to appreciate that basic concept. But I saw it time and time again in my own company. While Mikes and the other wannabes invested their lives in telling others what had to be done, I watched real leaders focus first on the why and the how—often doing it with stories that compelled.

Sound ridiculously simple? Maybe—but ask yourself how often you've been exposed to real influencers in your life. Did they convince you with the hard facts or via the emotional channels of the heart first?

Leadership guru Simon Sinek codified this far better than me in his book *Start with Why*. If you're serious about your career, it's a very worthwhile read.

Oh, and Roosevelt? It can be said that 15-minute speech back in 1933 changed the course of history. No Mike could have saved us then—but a leader did.

STRAIGHT TALK

Transformational Leadership implies an ability to inspire and to engage—accessing the heart and head to bring about sustainable change. Transactional Leadership is not really leadership at all—it's management. It implies a quid pro quo relationship in which I reward you if you perform.

Both have a place in the corporate world and in most careers, but only one sustains an organization and can compel a movement. Understand the why and you are one step closer to becoming a difference maker. Effectively convey the why and you are there.

COMMUNICATION

"The single biggest problem in communication
is the illusion that it has taken place"
~George Bernard Shaw

When I was 25 I sat in big convention halls awed by orators who I was convinced were the great communicators. By the time I was 35 I had begun to question that assumption. I watched highly articulate speakers leave the stage without any commitment from their audience—no followership on their bold vision. In the years that followed, I finally learned the truth. Those truths are captured in the chapters that follow.

EVERYONE IS IN SALES

"The key to successful leadership today is influence,
not authority."

~Ken Blanchard

Everyone in the business world—whether in accounting or research, whether a physician in an integrated network or a guy parking cars at the valet stand, whether sitting on the board at the local bank or running the meat department at the grocery store—everyone is in sales.

The challenge is most never realize it. In their mind they're an individual contributor or an information expert or a researcher—anything but sales.

"Sales are what that guy down at the used-car lot does—not me."

Wrong. Sales are synonymous with influencing others. Making a sale is the art of negotiation and it requires the capacity to learn more about others— not to simply speak at them. It is a skill set you must develop and hone for the rest of your career if you intend to thrive in your career—whether or not you are in the corporate world.

Now, contrast that with the foundation offered most when they walk off a college campus. A 2012 Harvard Business Review article stated that less than a quarter of the 479 accredited business schools in the United States offered a sales curriculum. Only 15 percent had either an MBA in sales or a curriculum considered sales oriented. Put another way, some 350,000 students walk off their college campus with a business degree each year while some 170,000 do so with an MBA. But only a small percentage have really been taught anything about sales.

Those figures are changing—dramatically. Each year more universities are embracing the fact that sales offer one of the best channels for employment—and the life skills that transcend the job.

My *"falling"* into a sales position in my first real job greatly changed my career trajectory.

In the years that followed I learned an effective communicator is first an effective salesperson—and that includes every schoolteacher, every fitness instructor, every interior designer, every ICU nurse, and every squadron leader that ever walked the earth.

STRAIGHT TALK

Anyone who expects to make an impact must understand the importance of selling his or her ideas. If your job requires you to communicate—and show me one that doesn't—get comfortable with it.

You will not thrive unless you embrace the simple notion that all of us—to varying degrees—must sell.

THE IMPORTANCE
OF QUESTIONS

"You can tell whether a man is clever by his answers.
You can tell whether a man is wise by his questions."
~Naguib Mahfouz

The final concurrence interview for the job that would become a career was conducted at the old Raleigh-Durham Airport a long, long time ago. I still remember the three-plus-hour drive across the state to get there (there was no way the company would invest in an airline ticket on me yet) and going through my prep notes as I sat in my car getting ready to go in. The selection process had been long and intense. And I knew I was very much a dark horse candidate.

No legitimate business pedigree. No sales background. But I had still managed to make it to the final round.

The ensuing meeting turned out to be a classic example of how sometimes knowing as little as possible can be an advantage—sort of the Forest Gump approach to corporate excellence.

Back then most of the people attempting to enter pharmaceutical sales were walking into an industry about to experience significant change. The era of the *"blockbuster"* new medicines was at hand. Companies were investing millions in bringing sales forces together that would optimize their investments. Marketing became a focal point, and a dramatically different selling model was sweeping much of the landscape. The latest was labeled consultative selling, but it was really a continuation of milestone work that dated back as far as the '20s and E. K. Strong's landmark book

The Psychology of Selling and Advertising. The interaction with the customer, experts reasoned, was a specific process and set of skills that could be learned, not just an instinctive "feel." Consultative selling carried it to another level. Stated simply, it challenged salespeople to develop and incorporate well-thought-out questions designed to build a deeper relationship with the customer.

Now the industry expected physicians to actually listen.

Against that backdrop I made my way onto the audition stage. I had chosen to pursue a job in pharma because I'd heard the pay was good and I had met one or two people in the industry. In other words, I had no vision, no plan, and no strategy.

My interview that fateful day revealed an unwelcome truth.

I knew next to nothing about business, particularly sales.

I had one advantage. I was a converted journalism major who had toyed with broadcasting as a backup; I could always talk. That carried me through at least a portion of the interview conducted by a district manager and a local field trainer. And then came what should have been my Waterloo. The manager paused, studied me for a few moments and asked me to role-play a sales call with his colleague. I was to sell the lamp that sat on a coffee table beside me. The only backdrop provided—the potential buyer was looking to match something in a Mediterranean motif.

I was at an impasse. I had literally never sold anything in my life—not cookies for the PTA, not seeds for the various grade school fund drives, not candy for the holiday Christmas pageant. Nothing. One would think that would be my biggest immediate challenge.

It wasn't.

My lack of selling instinct was overwhelmed by a greater fear. What was *"Mediterranean décor,"* and what the heck was I supposed to say about that?

I paused and in that moment a single ray of divine providence shone down on me. In retrospect I can say it changed the trajectory of my professional life. Faced with nothing to say I opted to ask my "client" a question. I didn't want to, but I had nothing.

"Sir, when you say Mediterranean, can you tell me a little more about that?"

My potential buyer said, *"Well, my wife is really big into Mediterranean and she wants me to pick up something for the living room."*

OK, still lost here.

"Yes sir, can you give me a bigger picture, when you say Mediterranean, what specifically would you be looking for?

"You know, muted colors—brown, oranges, grays—but something that accents the room." (Which, by the way, tells me today that it was debatable my interviewer knew much about design either.)

It's important to say that at that point in my life I cannot be completely sure I even knew where the Mediterranean was, but I at least understood a bit more about what colors might be needed—unfortunately, not enough to do anything with it.

I had no choice—I fought my natural instincts and I continued to ask questions.

"Something that accents the room." I answered, *"What other things do you have in the room?"*

Somewhere, somehow—magic occurred. I actually began to understand what the heck it was I was supposed to talk about. A half-dozen questions in, I could jump back on my *"go-to"*—talking.

Now it's critical to note that at the end of the role-play I had not really closed for action—something I was to learn was anathema for top salespeople. Nor can I say it was a particularly cogent presentation. But it was clear when it was over that the district manager was overjoyed. He saw someone he believed was instinctively asking questions to better understand customer needs, demonstrated active listening skills, and clarified and confirmed their understanding before simply presenting information. He was downright gleeful, as was the field trainer who was the other half of the simulation. Both took the time to point out I was one of the few who actually created dialogue—not just a regurgitation of mindless (and imagined) product features or benefits.

Apparently I was a natural—at least in their eyes. I smiled and nodded, accepting their compliments with the calm demeanor of someone who knew exactly what he was doing and why.

What a crock.

The truth was two things salvaged the interview for me. The first was my inherent lack of knowledge on what I was doing—both from a selling standpoint and as regards interior decorating. The second was that because

I knew so very little on both fronts I had no choice but to ask questions—a lot of them.

Those questions saved me. I got very lucky, winning a job I was probably not fully prepared to assume.

This was my first lesson in my corporate journey, and like many of the ones that followed; it took me years to truly appreciate it.

STRAIGHT TALK

Talking, for most of us anyway, is the easy part. Listening is not.

THE POWER OF STORY

"Imagination is more important than knowledge."

~Albert Einstein

It all began with a snowflake.

At 10 p.m. EST on the frigid night of April 14, 1912, Frederick Fleet and his shipmate Reginald Lee took their post as watch for their vessel as it sailed through the clear waters of the North Atlantic. The sea was like glass on this moonless night, and both were anxious for their two-hour post to end. There was coffee below, and the cold wind chapped their skin. Neither carried binoculars. It was rare that a lookout carried binoculars in those days. Fleet and Lee's was a big and powerful ship. There was nothing in the waters that could threaten save perhaps another ocean liner. Both men kept their eyes peeled on the horizon even as they chatted in a low voice.

Down below their captain had turned in for the night. Like his crew, Edward Smith was supremely confident in the powers that technology and modern engineering had brought to naval travel. Several years before he had proclaimed he *"could not imagine any condition that would cause a ship to founder. Modern shipbuilding has gone beyond that."*

Captain Smith was wrong.

At 11:40 that evening Frederick Fleet's eyes suddenly narrowed. There in front of them something huge suddenly loomed out of the darkness— blacker than the night and obscuring the stars that hung low over the horizon.

Fleet screamed into his radio, *"Right ahead, iceberg!"*

The ship's first officer, William Murdoch, gave the command to reverse engines and turn.

But it was too late. The ship scraped the massive mountain of ice on the starboard side, shearing vital compartments like paper torn by a jagged piece of barbed wire. And devastating tragedy followed.

Some three hours later the largest ocean liner in modern history broke in two and settled into a watery grave with over 1,500 passengers perishing with it. Approximately half that number survived the greatest nautical disaster of all time—the sinking of the Titanic.

The ship had received multiple wire warnings of ice in the area from other ships. They ignored them but not because of the conventional theory that White Star Line wanted to break a record for the inaugural voyage. The reality—icebergs were not considered a threat to ships of this size. There was no precedent for this kind of nautical accident. Those ships that had the misfortune of hitting an iceberg had never sunk.

And this was the mighty Titanic after all—a marvel of engineering. Widely proclaimed as unsinkable as it prepared for this, its maiden voyage. There was no need to slow their speed. There was no need to increase the watch. There was no need to even outfit Frederick Fleet or Reginald Lee with a set of binoculars.

The ship carried 20 lifeboats—more than the 16 maritime law at the time required. But even at full capacity the lifeboats could not account for the total number of passengers on board. Nor was the crew prepared to deal with the aftermath of the collision. Most of the lifeboats that fateful evening were deployed with far less than maximum capacity.

Chaos and madness had replaced arrogance.

The temperature of that black water was 28 degrees Fahrenheit—not survivable for more than 45 minutes. Only 13 survivors would be plucked from its frigid embrace. The remainder quickly slipped into hypothermia-induced cardiac arrest, likely dying even before the last remnant of the great ship sank into its black oblivion.

It would remain there undiscovered on the ocean's floor two-and-a-half miles below—for over 70 years. It was as if the Titanic and all those who died with it slipped away into the freezing darkness to be lost forever.

It was misguided faith in technology and arrogance from a great many that killed the Titanic.

A story a hundred years in the making and fraught with pathos—incredible triumph as the world watched the greatest example of modern innovation launch from its English birthplace, and then horrific tragedy as in its maiden voyage it fell victim to the dangers of the sea.

A simple story—one that teaches us of the dangers of misguided confidence, the risks of failing to prepare, and the unwillingness to listen. The Titanic was an avoidable tragedy. In the years that followed its sinking maritime law would change dramatically—procedures on board ships would become more stringent, North Atlantic iceberg patrols would be established, and international guidelines would be finalized.

So why does any of this have anything to do with your ability to thrive in the corporate world?

Well, imagine you've just been asked to offer a presentation on contingency planning for your department head. If you're like most you will assemble the obligatory PowerPoints, complete with reams of data that support your platform. Toss in a couple of cost analysis grids and a benchmark example, frame your talking points up against The Core Analytics from an earlier chapter, and you have a surefire successful presentation, right?

Maybe—maybe not. I've participated in literally thousands of group presentations, sometimes at the front of the room and sometimes as a member of the audience. It took me a while to begin to really think through what made some speakers incredibly influential and others painfully ineffective.

Until I began to appreciate **The Power of Story—the First Cardinal Rule of Communication.** It is something you must learn to embrace if you are ever to make the simple skeleton of The Core Analytics become more than just a few questions to build a presentation around.

Stated simply, it is the narrative that captures the heart, not just the facts that support the conclusions.

Let's go back to your presentation on contingency planning. You cover the meeting room with data to support your recommendations using every graph to demonstrate the cost effectiveness of your alternatives. And if you're like most, you'll find out very quickly that sometimes the most well-founded argument can be quickly lost on your audience.

Why? Because we are not hardwired to simply synthesize numbers and reach conclusions. Even the most logical and traditional *"left-brain"* thinker will respond to a broader approach.

So let's say that instead of simply dropping the numbers on your audience you take a different tack. You tell them the story of a company so enamored with its strategic plan and so blinded by its own technology that it could not fail. You offer warnings about the capacity to listen and to adapt that foolproof strategy.

But instead of regaling with charts, you introduce them to Captain Smith or Frederick Fleet. Perhaps you equate that new competitor less with a brand profile and more with a hundred million pounds of ice somewhere in the dark and forbidding seas of the North Atlantic.

Maybe that dedicated customer base becomes more than a faceless populace. Perhaps it becomes a screaming mother and a helpless child destined to sink into an icy grave.

That contingency plan—imagine how much more compelling it might be when you equate it to lifeboats that fail to save anyone.

The market research study you hope to pitch—wonder if it might resonate even more when you compare it to ship look-outs so convinced of their brand's invincibility that they never carry an optic on reality?

You paint a picture that does more than inform, it engages your audience.

I carry on my key chain a tiny sliver of bituminous coal. It was salvaged from the wreckage of the Titanic. It reminds me every time I walk in front of a group that their heads may nod but it's their hearts I hope to hook.

STRAIGHT TALK

The Power of Story is the First Cardinal Rule of Communication. Compelling presentations are made by the metaphors and similes that help vividly express your points by engaging the often misunderstood right brain of your audience—the creative side that hungers to be aroused but often slips into the shadows in the corporate world.

The very best communicators are first great storytellers.

THE POWER OF STORY
Part Two

"If history were taught in the form of stories,
it would never be forgotten."

~Rudyard Kipling

It took me a very long time to reconcile The Power of Story in the business world. I had entered a place of linear thinking and hard data, of sales numbers and sometimes maddening analysis.

There didn't appear to be a lot of storytellers here.

And then one day I found myself in a crowded auditorium, watching a highly competent leader talk a group of colleagues into an information-induced coma that brought the meeting to an end. By the fifth data slide the game was lost.

I asked myself why? And what could I learn from that very painful experience?

The answers I've carried with me for a very long time.

Whether you're presenting to a customer, to your company's board, or to the local Boy Scout troop, whether you're talking to the guy on the assembly line or your chief executive officer—here are **The Story Tenets** you need to understand if you plan on becoming a person of influence:

> • **People want you to excite their passions.** They need
> you to do more than engage their left brain—the logical
> and ordered world that flows past them every day.
> They want you to hook the right brain—the creative,

emotional piece that excites and invigorates. You grab an audience in the first 60 seconds or you lose them forever. You have one minute to clutch their hearts and to hold their minds. And that begins with getting the lid off as regards their attention and focus. The hook is everything.

• **We all want to hear a story.** We want to be entertained. We hunger for someone to do more than inform us. We want someone who will engage our senses. Scare us, surprise us, shock us, motivate us— just don't bore us.

• **No story resonates without conflict—without a struggle.** Struggle engages us—it compels us to want to listen. The first two questions in The Core Analytics set the stage to introduce the pain points, whether you're talking about a novel or your presentation to your boss. If you are a strong storyteller you will use those questions to effectively introduce the "bad guy"—the challenge that must be overcome. That can be anything from a downward market share, to a competitor bent on your destruction, to a market condition that threatens your business, to an iceberg in the middle of the North Atlantic; but until you communicate the point of conflict—nothing happens. Nothing.

• **PowerPoint presentations can kill you.** Wordy slides and reading to the audience is the best way on the planet to murder a story. I remember watching one of the brightest people I ever met walk through 10 slides that had a minimum of 40 words on each, and enough graphs to plot the theory of relativity. He lost his audience in the first five minutes. Bets were taken on how many in the audience would break for the bathroom as an excuse to try and regain their sanity. Painful.

• **In every great story there will be a hero— a protagonist.** That hero may be an idea, it may be an individual, it may be an initiative, but without the struggle and the knight on the white horse that comes to the rescue there is no story. And yes—questions three, four, and five in The Core Analytics offers you the opportunity to weave that narrative. The very best tell their story in such a way that it compels the audience to listen.

• **Logic may set the stage but it is emotion that wins the day.** Even the most analytical of us responds to a story that engages the senses and appeals to our souls. The Greek philosopher Aristotle spoke of the three components of persuasion—ethos (credibility), logos (logic and data), and pathos (emotions). The first two set the stage but it is the latter that brings it all home.

Your ability to weave stories into how you communicate with others is far more important than you may realize. The Core Analytics are a business tool that can help offer you a framework on which to build a presentation or an analysis but the skeleton will not carry the day.

For that you have to appeal to the heart, which extends far beyond traditional business presentations. Hard numbers might validate, but it is the story that will resonate.

So, how many people in corporate actually become outstanding storytellers? The ones that become the most influential—regardless of their level in the organization.

Show me the leader most highly respected in your department and I'll bet you they are effective communicators. Point out the person who commands an audience and I'll guarantee they appreciate The Power of Story. And if your role is to in some way influence change in others (which is virtually every job you will ever hold) then your ability to weave a compelling story is virtually mandatory.

I couldn't resist one last illustration of why The Power of the Story is integrated into our DNA. We began the narrative around the Titanic by saying it all began with a snowflake, and yet the night of April 14, 1912, was a cloudless one. Scientists tell us that snowflake probably fell some 10 to 15,000 years before—somewhere in the frozen north of the Artic Circle where it was compressed with billions of other flakes into millions of pounds of ice that formed a glacier. That glacier eventually grew so large that a single chunk broke away and began to float aimlessly toward the channels that would someday include the greatest ship of its time.

A collision with destiny some might say.

I have always found it ironic that at almost the same time as that snowflake fell the world was entering the final stages of the last great ice age—the Pleistocene period. And archaeologists tell us that it was possibly a break in the glacial fields that allowed a small handful of nomadic hunters to make their way across what is now the Bering Strait from Asia onto the North American continent, likely following the herds of mammoth and other megafauna. Nomadic hunters with only their strength and their instincts to survive a strange new land so harsh that it is scarcely imaginable today. But our ancestors enjoyed one advantage—the saber toothed lions, the short-faced bears, and the great mastodons did not.

I picture those brave souls gathered around a fire, seeking solace and comfort from others in a harsh world that threatened every day to end their lives. Their language was likely crudely formed. There was no written word. That was at least 8,000 years in the future.

But they could learn from one another.

And they did learn.

They did it in the most powerful way possible.

They told stories.

STRAIGHT TALK

"Once upon a time..." Remember those four words when you were young - the tapestry of memories that stream from a simple bedtime story? Or perhaps the novel that captivated your adolescence... or the movie that haunts you still? It is story that links us as a people. It is The Power of Story that will accelerate your career.

THE MAGIC
OF AUDIENCE
ENGAGEMENT

"Alone we can do so little: together we can do so much."
~Helen Keller

I was part of the generation that grew up watching Johnny Carson on *The Tonight Show*. Like millions of others I marveled at the ease with which the King of Late Night brought me into a world very different from my own. Here was an ultra-smooth host that invited me to take a seat on the couch beside Ed McMahon each weeknight and to laugh like an insider as the parade of celebrated guests dropped by my living room. They say no one ever did it better. Certainly no one perfected the art form quite as well until Carson came along.

In the years since other giants continued to build on and expand that platform. Oprah Winfrey crafted an empire, single-handedly reframing the definition of a talk show. Radio icon Howard Stern literally made his listening audience a part of the cast. Ellen DeGeneres is a virtuoso, a comedic genius who dances with us, plays practical jokes on us, and makes us laugh and then cry and then laugh again.

I believe there are points of commonality that connect some of the very best; the power of the medium is headquartered in the unique ability of the host to make the viewer a part of the event, not just an observer.

Take a close look at today's morning talk shows. Whether we realize it or not, we are all guest stars in the larger event. From the games to the trivia questions to the audience question-and-answer, it's clear producers have come to recognize that removing some of the traditional barriers that separate observers and the *"talent"* have evaporated.

One could make the argument that critical ingredient is not limited to just talk shows.

Have you ever attended a Garth Brooks concert or been a part of the Justin Timberlake madness that sweeps a convention center? There is an almost supernatural experience that sweeps over an audience when the magic meets the music.

There's a reason Lady Gaga coined the term for her fans *"Little Monsters."* The best of the best involve the crowd. The others simply perform for the crowd.

It took me a long, long time to fully appreciate what I call the **Second Cardinal Rule of Communication** and the correlate to **The Power of Story.**

To thrive in your corporate journey you must embrace **The Magic of Audience Engagement.** The story will hook them but you will not hold them unless your listener becomes a part of the narrative.

The first truly influential trainer I ever met on the subject of public speaking was a master in getting his listeners involved. His premise was remarkably simple. Engage the senses and you engage the heart. Engage the heart and the head will follow.

When he walked to the front of the room the very first time he carried with him an empty glass and a pitcher of water. He started to speak and then sputtered a time or two before he apologized for his scratchy voice and started to pour himself a glass of water.

The audience laughed when the water seemed to mysteriously pour over the sides and onto the floor, clattering with the chunks of ice around his feet. An awkward silence followed and many of us wondered why this guy was up in front talking about the power of public speaking.

He waited a few seconds before he said something I never forgot.

"You've just been offered your first lesson on becoming an effective communicator." He held his glass up high and removed a small cover of Saran Wrap that covered the top and added, *"Nothing happens with an audience until you find a way to get the lid off."*

He laid the glass down and held the wet wrap out for all of us to see before he said, *"And believe me, every audience you ever encounter between now and the end of your career—whether it's one person or one thousand—will have barriers to effective communication. You may not know what they are. They may not know what they are...but they are there. It's up to you to figure out how to remove them."*

I could not fully appreciate how true that one statement was at the time but I would soon discover it for myself. Whether I carried a pitcher drawn from the Well of Knowledge or from the birdbath in my backyard, no one really felt obliged to listen to what I had to say unless I found a way to get the lid off as regards their attention and interest.

Thought-provoking questions. Provocative challenges. Check backs to ensure understanding. Mirrored inquiries that play off of one participant's comments and go back to the group to vet understanding and buy-in. I was to learn that how I planned my opening and how I planned my questions in many ways trumped the content.

The objective most of us carry into any group presentation is usually this: What's the big idea I want the listeners to come away with?

An equally key objective should be: How am I going to get the group involved in arriving at the big idea?

Translation: You are preparing for an interactive story session when you plan a presentation. You play a role. Your audience plays a role. Prepping your part requires more than learning just your lines. It demands you plan for how you will elicit lines from your audience. And that is what separates good public speakers from great public speakers.

There is, in the theater world, a term that describes this phenomenon. It's called The Fourth Wall, and that term represents the mythical dimension we, as audience members, look at when we view a stage. There is of course the back wall and the two sides. The one we look through from the front is invisible. The Fourth Wall represents the lens that separates us from the actors. That line of separation is there for a reason, and in much of the world of entertainment is critical. We are looking at a world playing out in front of us as silent observers.

When theater directors choose to remove that barrier they call it *"breaking the fourth wall,"* and there are masters in the world of comedy and entertainment that lead that charge. Think of the late Robin Williams and his running dialogue with his audience, singer Josh Groban and his repartee with fans, or any country singer on the planet and the act that keeps them in front of rabid crowds.

In the movie, *Ferris Bueller's Day Off*, the lead character had a running commentary with the camera. His famous lines, *"Life comes at you pretty fast. If you're not careful you might miss it,"* became a part of cinematic lore; sage advise to a personal friend who was watching from just out of camera sight—you and me. For the more devious version of the same approach see Frank Underwood in *House of Cards*!

We are not bound by the laws of good theater in the corporate world and yet a great many speakers construct their own version of a Fourth Wall, satisfied to talk from behind an invisible Saran Wrap barrier that forever separates them from the other partner in their presentation—the audience. They construct those barriers by not engaging the listeners, not responding to the cues that are there, and never managing to stimulate the senses of those who will dictate whether the speech is successful or an abject failure.

A number of years back I was able to join a group of senior sales leaders for a breakfast meeting with football icon Lou Holtz, who had joined us as a keynote speaker for the sales force that day. If you've never heard Holtz, you've missed the opportunity to hear a truly great speaker—motivational, glib, and wildly entertaining. But beyond all of those positives, I learned something else in our breakfast meeting that subtly distinguished him from a great many others. He spent the better part of our hour together asking questions about our company, our strategy, and our vision for the future. Then he asked for names of salespeople who exemplified excellence, dutifully collecting the names on a pad in front of him. I was impressed but frankly unclear on what he might do with the reams of notes when he was only going to be onstage for 45 minutes and was speaking to an audience of several thousand in less than three hours.

And then I watched a maestro weave every name, every example of greatness into his story. When he talked about personal goal setting and the determination to realize those objectives, he did more than talk about his journey—he referenced people within our organization who had done the same. When he talked about overcoming seemingly hopeless obstacles, he recounted his struggles and then likened them to people within our company who had done the same thing. The representatives in that audience began to hear peers' names mentioned by this nationally known figure as easily as they might if Holtz worked alongside them in the field.

The effect was mesmerizing.

And I walked away with an appreciation that involving the audience might be the single most effective way to not just get the lid off for your listeners but also to sustain their interest.

Perhaps even more important, it taught me that I could do that if the group was five people or 5,000. It might be easier with the smaller audiences because questions and general give-and-take makes for a simpler vehicle to engage, but with a little extra planning any speaker can get their audience involved.

STRAIGHT TALK

The Fourth Wall may be an invisible barrier but it is very real. **The Magic of Audience Engagement** is the **Second Cardinal Rule of Communication.** Combined with The **Power of Story** they form an amazing foundation.

And the thread that runs through both of them —**The Capacity to Listen.**

Understand these core elements and maybe you'll be able to strip that Saran Wrap away forever.

GAMBLERS, COPS, AND CON MEN

*"The most important thing in communication
is hearing what isn't said."*

~Peter Drucker

Early in my career I was partnered on a challenging project that offered me an opportunity to learn and to grow. And it turned out the growth had absolutely nothing to do with the work assignment. It had everything to do with the person I was assigned to work with.

He was bright, he was intuitive, and his career was ascending. And from the very first moments of the very first day I didn't trust him. For the life of me I couldn't figure out why.

Everything he said was well informed. He enjoyed a strong reputation in the company. He worked hard and he was sharp. And I left our first meeting with a level of unease I had seldom experienced.

In the weeks that followed and over the course of multiple meetings I began to understand why—but only obliquely. And it went back to what he didn't say versus what he did say.

My new workmate had a tendency to fidget when someone else was speaking. I would watch his legs bounce underneath the table as if he were ready to pounce. Nothing wrong with that, just a high-energy type, I guess. But I also noticed his eye contact often broke off quickly with others and he would return to his notes when the subject veered from what he wanted to talk about.

I watched him shut off conversations with others, sometimes with a slight wave of his hand and other times with only a cocked eyebrow, and over time I finally put a finger on something that—until that point—I had a very shallow appreciation for.

The powerful message of body language.

Years later I picked up one of the most valuable books I've ever read. It's what I consider to be the definitive guide on nonverbal communication. Written by former FBI special agent Joe Novarro and Princeton University's Marvin Karlins, PhD, *What Every BODY is Saying* helped me appreciate that there was a science behind my very elementary observations, and it was something I had only a passing understanding of.

Novarro was a counter-intelligence specialist trained in interpreting body language. He shares his principles of nonverbal interrogation and how our nation's best investigators apply those lessons every day.

Reading this book opened my eyes to the one source of ultimate truth that each of us carries within—the limbic portion of our brain. That's the portion that reacts to the world reflexively, our emotional core. It is a hardwired survival center that dates back to the *"freeze, flight, or fight"* coding of our ancestors.

In the sales world you are trained to read your customer, but much of the read speaks to content versus context. The higher advanced neocortex part of our brain has no problem in intellectually interpreting the world around us. It is that level of higher thought that distinguishes our species. The neocortex analyzes, it interprets, and it synthesizes information.

It also does one more thing.

It lies.

The neocortex is capable of deception.

But the limbic—ah, the limbic, that ancient defense mechanism that kept us alive back in the primeval days—is not quite so discerning. It is a *"hot switch"* that is much more difficult to disguise.

Imagine a poisonous snake has just been dropped on the floor in front of you. Your limbic brain reacts instantaneously. You scream, you jump away, your blood pressure skyrockets and sweat pours from you as you try to extricate yourself from the danger.

The neocortex (which means new brain) might begin to guide you to next steps, but in that first few seconds it's safe to say your visceral response is driven by the limbic.

And much of your nonverbal communication comes from the limbic.

Translation: Your words may sing sweet praise but your body could be saying, *"no, no, no."*

The limbic brain, Novarro says, *"is the holy grail of body language."*

And in the corporate world it is sometimes the unsaid that carries the day.

But before I could pull the magnifying glass up and start better understanding the nonverbal communication of those around me, the mirror forced me to ask some tough questions of myself. The book made me appreciate my own body language and some of my tendencies, which were not always conducive to true two-way dialogue.

I had always relied on the power of the spoken word as the major factor in communication—a very shortsighted view. But when I began to understand body language I began to grow more effective in inspiring two-way dialogue, in understanding more completely other people's views, and in moving beyond simply *"what was said."*

It helped me ask better questions. It helped me to listen with my eyes and not just my ears.

And I still have a very, very long way to go.

Incidentally, some of the very best in reading body language can be found in the vocations outlined in this chapter's title.

In business even a basic understanding can help us appreciate the behaviors that compromise our effectiveness. It also reinforces the potential limitations of two of the most common communication mediums at our disposal in the corporate world—the telephone and the computer; rich conduits but arguably never as valuable as the old-fashioned face-to-face meeting.

I can remember to this day approaching a professor back in college whose opinion I wanted to seek out regarding a choice of major. This particular individual was an incredible classroom instructor—engaging, funny, and informative. I looked forward to his lectures and truly enjoyed the way he taught. I figured getting him at the end of class and asking him for two minutes of perspective might be a good play. And I watched an amazing transformation from the glib "onstage" persona to someone who offered terse responses and demonstrated little to no interest in me as an individual.

But what really bothered me was the nonverbal. He was more concerned with arranging his papers, checking his schedule, and even straightening his tie than in offering me even an ounce of opinion. Our conversation lasted less than the two minutes I had hoped for, and I lost my admiration for my favorite prof, not because of the content but because of his demeanor.

What he didn't say was devastating.

I was to watch little scenarios like that play out hundreds of times in the years that followed. In time I was finally able to connect the dots on the impact of the unspoken and powerful influence of body language, especially when I began to watch those leaders in my organization who were fluent practitioners in the art. And so I finally grasped there were two dimensions of articulate communication.

Much of human behavior is captured in the unsaid. Some of the practitioners in the previously mentioned career fields are not so much gifted with supernatural skills as they are keen observers of body language— the shift of an eyebrow, the glance upward, the subtle movement of the feet away from the individual they're talking to, the folded arms, or the movement of a hand to their chin.

Watch the next *World Series of Poker* and you will see some of the most astute practitioners on the planet.

If you believe that your success is dependent on your ability to work with people, then consider how much you really know about how to read them.

Maybe more important; what are the *"nonverbals"* you send out every day? Do they build relationships or do they tear them down?

Gamesmanship? Anything but—simply one more learning tool to increase your effectiveness.

Oh, and by the way, you will soon consider yourself an expert in TV crime shows and the various late night documentaries on unsolved cases.

If it were only that easy.

STRAIGHT TALK

The words are the easy part in the corporate world. It's the unsaid that is difficult to interpret. Become articulate there and you will enjoy a line of sight many can only dream of.

I THINK I GOT
SOMETHING TO SAY

*"There is nothing so annoying as to have two people talking
while you're busy interrupting."*

~Mark Twain

I was hired into the corporate world on something of a fluke. When words failed me I stumbled into my salvation. It only took me another 10 years to fully appreciate what the experience should have taught me at the time.

You cannot be a person of influence if you don't take the time to listen to those around you, appreciate their viewpoints, tap into their strengths, and demonstrate true empathy for what is important to them. Your foundation is built on credibility and not on what you think you know.

And so, like many of the life lessons that had to be pounded into my head, this one carried me back to that first very lucky job interview and my stumble into a sales position all those years before.

It was the questions that were my lifeline. But it was the silence that saved me. The brief flash of patience that allowed me to actually shut up and allow my environment to teach me.

I've been able to watch an interesting transformation in health care over the last 35 years, and I am reminded of it every time I go out into the field to work with a sales representative. In the early '80s the majority of physicians in the United States were truly autonomous health-care providers. Their decisions driven by their own compass—the influencers outside their office were limited.

That's changed dramatically over the last several decades. The rise of managed care, the Affordable Care Act, payer demands, employer pressures, and health-care reform in general has transformed the role of the typical doctor. Today—whether they like it or not—most physicians are corporate employees. And that is very, very different from what a great many believed they were signing up for.

Many of the ratings and scorecards they are accountable for mirror the rest of the corporate world. Today, those metrics can determine their pay, their jobs, and their future. Prospering in it requires a level of organizational savvy many have had to carefully cultivate.

Here's an example of the challenges wrought: A few years back a study was conducted to assess the amount of time it takes for physicians to interrupt their patient when they sit down in their first consultation and the patient begins to talk.

The answer was shocking.

Twenty-three seconds.

Twenty-three precious seconds from when the patient begins to tell their story to when the doctor breaks the narrative. When I first read that figure I was shocked. But then I thought about my life and how I sometimes conducted business, and I realized it wasn't atypical. In fact in many cases I probably beat that figure in my interactions.

We all have work to do—especially today's physician. You don't see the required number of patients, you don't hit the mark on your performance metric, and your salary could suffer. Time—as they say—is money.

Exactly the same dilemma I face in my busy world, and my logic for cutting conversations short is just as sound. My rationale (if I were to be completely honest in justifying my mistakes)— *"I'm busy. I know what I'm doing. Let's get on with it!"*

When there is a pause in the action (or the dialogue) my tendency is to strike—with my own views. Who's comfortable with silence? We rush to fill the seconds with words. It might be inane babble and it might totally extinguish real dialogue but let's get going.

But narrative, I think, may be everything when it comes to real communication. We are hardwired to learn not so much with our left brain—the logical, linear thinker that assesses data and spits out interpretation—but with the right brain—the emotional and creative side that truly captures the vividness of the world around us.

I saw that countless times in the area of sales as a manager before I truly could grasp it. We literally invested millions in training succeeding generations of sales representatives—process, mechanics, and steps to the effective call—before I began to understand it was those few who could tell a compelling story that actually were the most successful.

And more important, they were able to allow those they worked with to tell theirs too.

Back to my colleagues—those physicians who have been thrust into the corporate world. It's interesting to me that so many medical schools have recognized the increasing power of narrative, even in the face of a much more demanding corporate environment for many doctors. Today a majority of the centers that turn out the newest wave of physicians now include courses in the humanities. When I entered the health-care world that was almost unheard of.

I believe that 23-second window may grow in the years to come.

STRAIGHT TALK

The failure to listen is deafening. It swirls around us in the corporate world—even as the storm grows louder. But for the few who understand its power there is refuge from the gales. The best listeners are usually the best learners. No organization will thrive without a handful of world-class experts in this advanced communication skill set.

THE PRINCIPLE OF HIGHER GROUND

"If you would lift me up you must be on higher ground."
~Ralph Waldo Emerson

Allow me to tell you one more little story—four different versions in fact.

It's a hot August day high in the Appalachian Mountains and a small group of fellow corporate hikers has stumbled on a river that meanders beside our trail. It's a relatively wide body of water but slow moving. The temperatures are in the mid-90s and our group has been keeping the same torrid pace that is common in corporate since the break of day. Our leader announces it's time for a rest and each of us is more than ready for an unplanned swim. We toss off backpacks and hiking shoes and wade into the dark, cool waters. A couple of our more adventurous peers climb up on large boulders that jut out of the water so they can dive in, hoping to impress perhaps one of several supervisors who remain on the sandy beach to stay on their cell phone. (Hey, no allegory can be complete without a cell phone or at least one or two Toadies.)

Suddenly one of the supervisors on shore stands and calls out in his most authoritarian voice, *"All right, everyone out of the water and NOW."* He stands and stomps his feet, pointing toward several who look like they are ignoring his direction. *"Billy,"* he continues, *"If you don't get out of the water this second you are getting a disciplinary letter. I mean it."* The group looks at one another and a majority begins to swim toward shore. Billy dips under the water. He knows he will have at least three verbal warnings before his manager can write him up anyway.

Now rewind. The same group in the water and the same games underway. This time the same supervisor stands and rushes toward the water, yelling, *"Break time is over. We all need to be out of the water in the next three minutes. No exceptions."* He glances toward Billy and says, *"I mean everybody, Billy."* The supervisor glances down at his watch and adds, *"My watch is ticking, team. NOW."* Our swimmers exchange wary glances. Billy rolls his eyes. There is a slow and resigned movement in the direction of the beach, though at least two team members, who have found a nice sunning spot on the rocks, seem less inclined to give up their position.

Now rewind again. Same group in the water. Same supervisor on shore, but this time he stands and announces in his most official voice, *"Alright I want everyone to begin to swim toward shore and I am going to check your progress with my trusty stopwatch."* He glances toward the laggards on the rocks and adds, *"And everybody needs to be at that log over there in the next 30 seconds."* He points to a large oak partially submerged in the water and only 30 feet from shore. *"I want the lines straight here, team. Important we get this right."*

And now rewind for the final scenario. Our supervisor stands and rushes to the edge of the water and yells to our swimmers, *"Team, I just got word that we've had a major thunderstorm to the north."* He points to the black clouds that drape the mountain to our right and adds, *"We have flood waters coming down this mountain and they're coming fast. We have to clear this beach and we need to clear it now!"* He moves to some of the swimmers who are closest to the sandbar he's standing on and begins to pull some of those nearby toward him before he dives into the water himself, grabbing less skilled teammates and guiding them toward land. He yells, *"We have our packs up on the trail. There's an overhang where we can wait out the storm, maybe grab some lunch. Let's move, crew."* The rock climbers are already in the water. Billy is setting what may be a new outdoor record for the freestyle.

Four different vignettes, each focused on a small group in the middle of a river who someone wants to move out of the water.

The early scenarios represent traditional command and control approaches. The first is *"Do it because I said so."* Some might call it coercion. Billy certainly would.

The second is not appreciably different—another variation of the *"C and C"* style. Little explanation on why action is needed but perhaps less coercive.

Were they effective? Well, at least some of the swimmers got out of the water. I've watched a lot of *"influencers"* who used a pretty similar approach in trying to affect movement from others. For that matter, I've watched a lot of salespeople do much the same. Tell, tell, and then tell some more.

The third scenario is arguably the most common approach to affecting change you will ever see in the corporate world, particularly as regards traditional managers. Micromanage your way to success. Attach as many grids as you can to the activity and your people will respond. It's a variation (some would say a bastardization) of the old *"inspect what you expect and expect only what you are prepared to inspect"* approach. It can and often does have value. I came up in a system that often relied on it and I believe there is inherent benefit, but it can stifle an organization and make *"activity for activity's sake"* the end rather than the means to an end.

The old quote, *"You cannot manage an army into battle, you can only lead them there,"* comes to mind when I think about our intrepid swimmers and affecting sustainable movement.

Which take us to the final scenario; the one that compels people to take action because it makes clear that taking action is to their mutual benefit. More important, it points out the risk associated with doing nothing at all. The most effective influencers recognize that creating dissatisfaction with the status quo can engage people far more effectively than simply tell, tell, tell or scream, scream, scream.

The difference between the middle of the river and higher ground represents the productive tension the best leaders I've ever met understood was the separator between good and great. Just like Roosevelt in 1933, they had the unique capacity to stimulate others to want to move, not simply comply.

They embrace the Power of Why.

In time I realized that space between status quo and higher ground was precious territory, easy to talk about but tough to traverse.

I found the same phenomenon when I worked with our very best salespeople. The narrative was most powerful for customers when we could do more than paint the picture of what higher ground could mean for them—but also help them understand the why and how of getting there—especially when contrasted with the consequences of simply holding onto the status quo.

The Principle of Higher Ground might seem to be common sense. Surely situations like the ones offered in our first three scenarios don't happen in the corporate world, right?

Don't kid yourself.

They happen every day, and in fact the *"line up and get out of the water"* analogy likely greatly exceeds all others. Taking the time to explain the *"why"* behind new initiatives or programs is often overlooked and/ or consciously omitted by leaders. But the why is everything as regards building consensus—as regards building commitment.

Why omit the why? Here are a few reasons I've seen companies/leaders use to justify not offering enough insight to affect positive change:

> • They (employees) can't handle the prospects of (in our little scenario) floodwaters. It will panic the masses. Better to keep them in the dark.

> • They won't understand. Who really appreciates that an upstream storm could raise water levels over 15 feet inside of five minutes?

> • They won't care. There are a lot of intangibles that effect downstream runoff. Many of the people in the water have heard about floods before. It won't make any difference.

> • Some of them will believe it won't affect them anyway. We have some savvy swimmers out there. Many of them could swim through a typhoon.

Our little allegory is exaggerated of course. The reality is a great many default to a *"Tell"* approach because it's simply expeditious.

Building transparency begins with trust; trust that others, when handed objective information, will treat it appropriately.

STRAIGHT TALK

The Principle of Higher Ground—of helping others to align around the need for change—isn't always easy to execute. The most influential leaders I've ever met understood people don't simply move because you want them to. They move when they understand it is in their best interest to change. That speaks to the power of productive tension—productive movement.

I've watched sales professionals transform the Higher Ground Principle into incredible selling prowess, and leaders who embraced it become persons of true influence.

If you understand the power of transparency you can move mountains. Trust is an amazing catalyst. Its grandfather is truth.

LEARNING

"Wisdom begins in wonder."
~Socrates

The ancient Greek philosopher's statement about the foundation for true genius has never been more real in this world in which information flows as readily as water from a million different fire hoses. But like a puppy bloated by one too many trips to the water dish, so do many of us mistake the accumulation of information as the accumulation of real knowledge.

And so a great many people on the career trail die of hunger—drunken with information while starved for learning.

I believe a very small percentage of career trekkers really embrace the notion of learning. No, not the commitment to classroom study or even the dogged determination that helps us attain that advanced degree or master a trade—that's prescribed learning that carries a carrot at the end.

I'm talking about something more; the inherent curiosity that makes us a student of life—that makes ideas a powerful part of our makeup. I've often wondered if many still suffer from that chapter in our lives when learning was foisted on us; the teaspoon of information that was bitter to swallow for many and always carried with it a score that dictated our grade—the class rank—and our place in the educational hierarchy.

The effect is like the one on the overweight 40-something-year-old who still has pangs of misery from the laps he used to run at football practice—I did it when I HAD to do it. Not going to do it now.

And after all, it takes work to learn. We live in a world today where there are a lot of options to real learning—most of them requiring far less effort. Information is everywhere. Easily obtained and with a modicum of energy expended.

But I came to appreciate that access to data or facts does not equate to learning, just as knowledge does not translate into skills or skill development.

And there is tragedy there because the curiosity that leads to learning is at the core of many of the most successful people I have met.

I know now that one of the things that sustained me was a passion for learning. I entered the business world with little to no background, hoping basically to someday make some money; arguably the worst motivation to pursue a job or a career but an indicator of how fortunate my early years were.

But I did have one advantage that many others did not—and many of them were far more advanced.

I was prepared to learn.

That became my salvation in a world of information and sometimes confusing conflicts. I began to appreciate the journey involved in acquiring knowledge and skills could be incredibly empowering. And was amazed at how much my environment was prepared to teach me if I would only take the time to watch and listen.

LOOKING BEYOND

"There are three classes of people: those who see, those who see when they are shown, those who do not see."

~Leonardo da Vinci

One of the highest compliments I was to receive during a very difficult first year with my company came from a field district manager who was trying desperately to make me into a salesperson. He stared at me after the latest long coaching session one day, smiled with what I suspect was a bit of resignation mixed in and said, *"You know what I like about you, Tim... you're like a sponge."*

It was a grudging compliment to be sure but I knew it was probably true. I had no problem in the area of *"willingness to learn."* It became a catalytic agent for me and I would need every ounce of it in order to survive.

For a long time I made learning my job responsibility my primary focus, but over time that changed too—dramatically. I came to appreciate that challenging myself beyond the parameters of the current role was in many ways far more important.

The job would eventually change. My thirst for learning would be quenched if I made it dependent on what the company paid me to do. But when I started to look a little more fully at the world around me, I began to embrace a more important truth—my mind was capable of more.

Robert Twigger, in an article in the digital magazine *Aeon* titled *Master of Many Trades* writes about the rise of the age of specialization and describes in clear terms a figure that plays prominently in the corporate world. He calls that person the monopath and characterizes him as follows: *"A person with a narrow mind, a one-track brain, a bore, a super-specialist, an expert with no other interests—in other words, the role-model of choice in the Western World."*

I've met him (or her) a thousand times over my many years—different name, different face, but the same person. Proud of their singular focus and unable to look beyond what I call their cubicle of responsibility. Remember the guy down the street who you want to avoid at every cocktail party because he'll pull you into a black hole that constantly goes back to his job? Or the lady who banters on about the wonders of real estate but can't carry on a conversation on anything related to any other area of the world around her?

But here is the real irony; we aren't hardwired that way. In fact the very evolution of the term Renaissance man is founded on the principles of an era when the *"perfected man"* was deemed a master of intellectual, artistic, and physical pursuits. *"Leonardo da Vinci,"* Twigger writes, *"was said to be as proud of his ability to bend iron bars with his hands as he was of the Mona Lisa."*

We are not obliged to stop learning when we leave school. Nor are we chained to one area of focus until the day we die. We can greatly expand our classroom, hence the definition for the term polymath; someone who is learned across a broad spectrum of areas and capable of applying that knowledge in richly creative ways.

I had no appreciation for that term over a part of my career and could never liken my broad areas of interest to the Renaissance period, but I came to appreciate that my ravenous desire to learn would someday become a difference maker.

One of the areas that always mesmerized me is history, and applying its lessons to broader learning fascinated me even more. Over time I began to be introduced to classic polymaths like Benjamin Franklin; a man we remember for his role in discovering the lightning rod but was also an author, historian, diplomat, physicist, and an agriculturist. Franklin represents the ideal modern polymath, capable of taking ideas from one field and applying them to innovations in another. Or Francis Crick, who first postulated the structure of DNA along with research partner James Watson, not because of his biology background but because of his foundational training as a physicist.

Twigger describes the power of broader thinking in a unique way. *"Invention fights specialisation at every turn. Human nature and human progress are polymathic at root. And life itself is various—you need many skills to be able to live it."*

You're entering a fast-paced highway when you walk into much of your corporate life—but it does not have to be a two-lane road; nor does it have to always run in the same direction as conventional thought demands it must. Some of the very best I have met somehow understood there can be a renaissance of thought in this sometimes rigid world.

They looked beyond.

Former South African president Nelson Mandela once said, *"Education is the most powerful weapon with which you can use to change the world."* Imprisoned for three decades for his anti-apartheid actions, Mandela never allowed himself to stop growing, pursuing six different degrees while behind bars. In time Mandela was to write the lessons learned into history.

We are not each destined to become a da Vinci, a Franklin, or a Mandela. But we can become so much more than we are. We possess at our fingertips the access to more knowledge than ever before in human history. And yet a great many people fail to fully leverage the gifts of what author Daniel Pink describes as the rise of *"the conceptual age."* In his book *A Whole New Mind*, Pink introduces the notion that traditional "left-brain" thinking in much of the corporate world is already becoming dated. The linear, logistic-driven skills of the past are being augmented by the more creative avenues associated with *"right-brain"* aptitudes—innovation, imagination, design, narrative, and emotional connections to others.

I came into business as a right-brain thinker who then adapted to what was largely a left-brain world. But in time I began to appreciate there was a place for whole-brain thinking. And that changed everything for me.

At the very center was a desire to learn.

I can't quantify what percentage of true learners walk the corporate trails, but I can attest to the staying power of those who are. It's up to you to decide if you're inclined to become one of them.

STRAIGHT TALK

Learning is your obligation—not the company you work for or the manager you report to. It will be a differentiator whether you choose to address it or not. You compete long enough and you will eventually line up against a learner, maybe for that promotion or the new role you've dreamed about.

Want to know the most important part of self-development?

Self.

NIFTY SHADES OF GRAY

"Knowing many things doesn't teach insight."
~Heraclitus

We live in an information-rich, insight-poor world, and no place can sometimes better epitomize that than the corporate world.

Data, numbers, and trends leak from our very pores. And it can give us a level of knowledge that dwarfs what we enjoyed even a decade ago.

It can also compromise our attention on what's most important, paralyze our ability to act, and overwhelm us—cluttering rather than clarifying.

Former secretary of state Colin Powell has been quoted as saying that he often wants only about 50 percent of the available information in order to make an important decision, arguing that too much data can interfere with a more important source for decision-making—his own intuition.

I once worked with a manager who was a master at *"crunching the numbers."* He could spit out a grid that would rival a NASA space launch trajectory analysis and could, at his leisure, quote data for any demographic or brand with equal abandon. He was deliberate, decisive, and absolutely resolute in every aspect of the business.

His direct reports and his peers were in awe of his prowess, as was I.

And his team was arguably one of the most inept I ever encountered when it came to execution. Oh, they could impress the heck out of you with a presentation, but when we began to talk about what we were doing with the analysis things got sticky.

It taught me something.

No interpretation of numbers is complete unless there is an important question that follows it.

"So what?"

There is often a misunderstood connector between analysis and action, and it is critical.

It's called insight.

Insight can best be described as the *"aha"* that follows analysis—the learning that goes a step further than the numbers. And it's much more than reciting trends or projecting the future. It's the living, breathing example of the application of human intuition and judgment, the step beyond the hard data that forces us to do more than interpret.

It demands we learn.

And that requires more than digesting or extrapolating numbers. The colleague I talked about earlier could juggle them all day, but if life (and business) was as easy as completing a math formula and then taking corrective action, much of the world's problems would be solved pretty quickly.

Here is what I learned from that experience. The analysis of data is an important first step to understanding a problem. It requires rigor and it requires discipline. But the gathering of insights is everything. And when you're gathering insight the world is not quite as black and white as we sometimes want it to be. That colleague was an "either-or" thinker, quick to pull a number and draw a conclusion. Ambiguity of any type confounded him—actually it infuriated him. His logic: if there was a problem then the solution must be there—and arrived at immediately. He was almost absurdly confident in everything he did. But the certainty he demonstrated masked blindness that crippled. He seldom asked others for input, checked his understanding, or allowed his team to really think through a problem or opportunity. He argued that doubt compromised effectiveness.

There were no allowances for shades of gray in the insight phase, and it blackened the world around him.

Over time I began to appreciate there was a place for gray in the corporate world, especially when you're assembling data and trying to interpret what it's telling you—when you're using it to develop ideas and plans for the future.

Years later I was to work with another leader who embraced the freedom of ambiguity in problem-solving and strategic planning. He in fact courted it. He engaged others, he challenged thinking, and he made certain there was rich dialogue as we conducted analysis and advanced to real insight.

What was the effect?

Creative, right-brain thinking permeated our meetings. We dared to ask ourselves the tough questions. We vetted potential solutions and often poked holes in them. Individual team members felt like they had a voice in the process. And when we finally decided on a plan, the doubts and concerns were replaced with a level of determination and commitment that bordered on zealotry. The gray was gone.

It took me years to appreciate the lessons learned.

STRAIGHT TALK

Analysis and insight gathering will have its share of muted shades. In fact, I think they are necessary. When we can traverse that land of uncertainty together we find the vibrant, bold colors of definitive action beyond the clouds.

Execution is an often talked about subject in the corporate world. I've come to realize that it is sometimes the work that precedes execution that can be most critical.

Analysis—Insights—Action. Like the colors of the rainbow the beauty is dependent on the eyes of the beholder. But one thing is certain, there is more to the spectrum than black and white.

INVESTMENT ADVICE

"Investing in yourself is the best thing you can do.
Anything that improves you own talents; nobody can tax it
or take it away from you."

~Warren Buffett

I came up in sales and if you are a salesperson you learn very quickly that there is a lot of *"hurry up and wait"* in our world. A top sales representative in the health-care industry might see 10 key customers a day, and if he or she is lucky, that might equate to no more than 30 minutes of actual interaction with a client.

"Windshield time" is a metaphor in the sales world that is used to represent the down time, the lack of productive hours—the dead zone. It's not true for all fields and all jobs, but in quite a few there is a lot of time that is wasted.

Granted, some of those hours should be spent in recharging and getting ready for when the game is in play. But for most of us, there is a lot of potential productivity that is spent in the mentally numbing place where we do nothing at all. We live in a world of information overload and insight deficiency. Even two hours a day can be converted into time you can use to enhance your overall skill sets.

But relatively few actually invest in their own self-development. And the number one reason typically cited for not doing that—the lack of time.

One of the things I had to learn through a series of missteps is that much of time management falls back to how well we can organize and prioritize our lives. In many cases it is less a function of how we manage the clock and more how well we manage our energy and our focus.

Some of the most successful people I've met in industry work hard to optimize what would otherwise be dead time, such as the empty hours spent in their car, on the train, or tucked away at some airport watching the latest broadcast of ESPN. And that doesn't mean simply filling nonproductive time with corporate busywork.

I believe we stoke our passions when we dare to invest in ourselves, when we actually feed that creative need to learn. We simply have to decide that giving back even a portion of our day to ourselves is OK.

There are more information tools available to us today than in human history—and only one click away on your computer. And yet many of them will never be accessed. We step over dollars to pick up the pennies of our everyday lives—and those pennies include the latest deadline, meeting, or project assignment.

Here's a small example from my career journey—a minor illustration of how even a simple investment can render amazing returns. Early on I began to appreciate that reading and comprehension was going to be a big part of my business life. I bought a book by Harry Lorayne and former NY Knick Jerry Lucas called *The Memory Book*, and was introduced to a system of recalling information far different from what I had learned in school. Lorayne was one of the first to make popular the magic of mnemonics—the process of attaching vivid pictures to everyday pieces of information. The concept is amazingly simple and equally powerful—basically shocking your mind to remember.

What I didn't appreciate at the time was that much of his techniques were borrowed from the ancient Greeks. In fact, the word mnemonics comes from the Mnemosyne—the mythological goddess of memory and the mother of the gods of the arts. The Greeks clearly differentiated between the natural and the artificial memory. The latter, they believed, had to be cultivated, and they recognized the importance of unleashing the creative mind in that process. Vivid imagery engages the brain in ways that simple rote memory skills can't.

And yes, if this summons strong connections to The Power of Story from an earlier chapter, it should. The right brain is the catalyst for a deeper level of communication and learning. The same principles that hook others when we are able to articulate compelling stories apply to the foundations associated with mnemonics and memory.

I had no appreciation for *"right-brain thinking"* when I purchased that little paperback, but I did begin to understand the power of the visual, design-oriented, contextual arena. At the time I considered them simple *"memory tricks,"* and they immediately helped me surpass the linear approach I had always used before to retain information. I worried a lot less about memorization and began to paint internal tapestries that were fun to create and challenged me to stretch a different part of my brain.

Harry taught me things I've carried with me for the better part of three decades. There are literally hundreds of books out there on building a better memory—but it's Lorayne and Lucas's that made a difference in my life. And if you don't believe the ability to retain information will be important in the corporate world you are kidding yourself.

By a similar token I also invested in a number of other courses—one of them driven by the fact that so much of my time was invested in covering books and articles. Simply reading and comprehending material was a tremendous time investment. Somewhere along the line I decided to accelerate that skill set.

I was to learn pretty quickly the way I read and absorbed information mirrored most everyone else's—visually scan left to right and repeat every word in your mind. What stunned me was when I began to understand that's about 20 percent of the pace at which you can actually comprehend information. And quickly repeating the words in my mind did not greatly change things. It was kind of like pushing peanut butter through a straw when the straw is a half-inch in diameter. You can expand the straw to a full inch but it's still peanut butter. I needed a better brand of peanut butter, not a new straw.

So I decided to relearn how I read. Bought speed-reading courses. Practiced. And promptly increased my speed three-fold while not compromising my retention (in fact, I suspect I improved it).

Don't rush to congratulate me. The principles of speed-reading are fairly well documented now. Like any skill, it can be improved with innovative principles and practice. But the giveback in my productivity was profound.

Will I ever break any records for either memory or for speed-reading?

Not likely—but I'm far better than I was when I walked off my college campus. And the price I paid for those little investments—less than a hundred bucks in total—amazes me when I consider the benefit derived. I coined a phrase that has stayed with me. I call it my **ROEI**. That stands for **Return on Energy Investment.** By my calculations, 10 hours and less than $100 changed how I was to study, learn, and retain information for the rest of my life—a staggering ratio.

AFTER ACTION REVIEWS

"The past is where you learned the lesson.
The future is where you apply the lesson."

~Dhiraj Raj

The military is oftentimes one of the very best sources to look to when assessing the successful execution of a mission. And it can offer insight to each of us as we embark on our corporate journey.

Here's another tip from an industry veteran that you might consider. Test it with your own company. More important, test it with yourself. It's based on a pretty simple formula I've seen repeated time and again.

Most organizations are *"all over"* the front end of an initiative, the rollout of a new plan, the introduction of a unique and novel strategy, the execution of an innovative initiative. We greet them with much fanfare and with the associated bells and whistles to trumpet them to the masses.

But we are very weak in going back after the fact and assessing impact.

Check that—we oftentimes never go back and objectively assess their impact.

We just move on to the next major movement. Corporations do it. Individuals do it. And as a result we fail to learn.

Not so in the military where the lives of men and women are often dependent on pinpoint accuracy and seamless execution. In that line of work you can't simply shrug your shoulders and wonder. You have to know if strategy and tactics led to a mission that worked exactly as planned. What's more, every mission is briefed before and after to painstaking degree, to correct as needed for the next sojourn.

It is a process well documented in books like James Murphy's Flawless Execution, one of the best I've ever read on the subject.

And what is the greatest potential transfer for the corporate world? Conducted well, After Action Reviews facilitate individual and company learning.

Remember your company's last major strategic thrust, that initiative that was going to drive you to unparalleled success, that tactical plan that was going to make you the undisputed brand or market leader?

Hmmm...yeah, kind of. But they sort of blur together, don't they? At best, they become a part of company lore, but seldom is there an accounting for their impact at more than a surface level. Most organizations have a short memory there. They simply move on.

The applicability for every individual is just as compelling. How often do you take the time to conduct your own personal After Action Review—an objective assessment of what did and did not work in your personal plan for that day, that week, that month?

The answer, for most of us, is *"not very often."*

No plan—no plan—is worth the paper it's printed on (or the screen on which it appears) unless there is as much diligence on the back end as there is on the front. The very best people I've ever worked with were incredibly diligent in conducting their own version of an After Action Review—either personally or with the people they worked with. More important, they had the courage to point out what did and did not work and why. Finally, they were willing to then amend their plans to make certain they worked better the next time.

One of the questions I've learned to ask both myself and others when we discuss business plans is, "What did we learn from our last After Action Review and how did that inform our current plan?"

Your career is like the stock market. There are competing forces that work to drive your value up while others attempt to force it down.

There is no status quo in our world, no notion of simply staying where you are. It's because your surroundings don't stay still. They evolve. You must evolve with them. You're either getting stronger or you're atrophying.

You're learning or you're not.

STRAIGHT TALK

Experience can be a phenomenal teacher. It's your decision on whether you allow it to be.

NO ONE MAKES IT
ON THEIR OWN

*"A mentor is someone who allows you to see the hope inside yourself.
A mentor is someone who allows you to know that no matter how dark the
night; in the morning joy will come. A mentor is someone who allows you
to see the higher part of yourself when sometimes it becomes hidden to
your own view. I don't think anybody makes it in this world without
some form of mentorship."*

~Oprah Winfrey speaking about her fourth-grade teacher, Mary Duncan

At some point in your career you will need to ask yourself two fairly simple but very tough questions:

- *"Do I have what it takes to really build a successful career?*
- *"Can I do this on my own?"*

I can only answer the second question for you. No.

I have never met a self-made success story. I don't believe they exist. Rambos are for the movies. You are foolish to believe your own skills and industriousness will sustain you. And if you take that approach you are robbing yourself of the true power of collaboration.

Whether you're two months or 20 years into your journey, take a step off the path. Find a mentor or two—individuals who have tread the trail ahead and can offer you insights you would not enjoy otherwise.

Now, here's the hard part. Quality mentors don't stand there in the corporate wilderness holding a sign over their heads inviting you to stop over for a cup of coffee. Sometimes you have to look for a bit.

Couple of hints on where to hunt: We all have a tendency to look at the same departments or divisions we are part of, but I can tell you some of the best selections may be outside your normal field of view. Remember—your mentor's role is not to become your career architect, but instead to be a real sounding board, a source of advice, and a confidant. They are providing counsel on something more than just how well you do your job. Your manager can train you on your job. A mentor needs to be much more.

A mentor can offer insight on organizational politics, decision-making in your organization, and practical perspective on the swirl of things whipping around you. One of my very best was always able to get me to stop, take a step back, and think in more objective terms. He was my own version of the Corporate Whisperer, and the lessons he offered transcended much of the formal training the company ever offered.

He was also the first to call out a blind spot where I often fell short. That subject was networking.

I've mentioned several times that my modus operandi early in my career was remarkably simple—and naïve. Work hard, demonstrate my value, and my efforts will be acknowledged and rewarded—in a utopian world, and if you're good, a reliable strategy. But remember, you are now part of a political ecosystem where your production can be washed over by a host of extraneous factors beyond your control.

And though many are reluctant to admit it, whom you know can be a career influencer.

The Whisperer helped me finally get beyond my own ego, and to realize my ability to broaden my sphere of influence required some additional hard work outside the normal white lines of the job. It meant cultivating relationships; it meant developing contacts; it meant looking beyond my own backyard and getting to know people.

And that frankly was not my strong suit. I prided myself on being fiercely independent and sometimes frowned on networking as *"playing the political game."*

In retrospect, an almost comically shortsighted view. Why I would believe a lone wolf could survive in a system that is dependent on collaboration is hard to explain.

You want a piece of advice from someone who walked the trail ahead of you? Make networking a core skill set. Get to know people, broaden your scope of influence, and establish reliable contacts to better understand your business and how it works.

More important, find a Whisperer—one person whose opinion matters to you. Someone you can trust. Select carefully. Watch the world around you before you make that selection. He or she is there and will always be there. You will never be able to identify a mentor by rank or title. Ask if you could talk to him or her from time to time. If this person is the real deal you will be able to tell by their response. The very best carry you far beyond the typical *"company speak."* In my opinion a mentor may be the most valuable contact you will ever make.

STRAIGHT TALK

Remember, you are not the first to blaze a career trail. Though no one can clear your path for you, not every step you take must be one of discovery. There are mentors out there who have charted at least a portion of the trail. They can help you thrive.

Learn from them.

CLOSING THOUGHTS

I wrote this book with the hope that it would offer advantages I had to earn the hard way.

The Compass was constructed from steps I stumbled over until my sense of direction finally became clear. It was only made powerful when I embraced the importance of **Personal Accountability**. My company changed as often as the wind, but I discovered I could set my sail on the consistency I built there.

True North.

Each of the other cardinal points of the Compass became an invaluable source of context when I finally learned to appreciate their importance.

Process helped me navigate the way work was conducted—or not conducted—and how I could fit into that larger whole.

People helped me understand the engine behind my company's success and how simple steps could enhance my ability to learn, collaborate, and grow.

Perspective became my career extender and helped me hold onto simple principles even when it seemed the world around me was spinning out of control.

My reliance on the four cardinal points helped me chart a course—even as I watched divisions and people sometimes be swept aside.

If you embrace their importance and seek to understand what they mean in your company, you have a foundation on which to build your own course.

But only a foundation.

Each of the Keys can carry you beyond.

Learning is the ship. It will separate you from the masses if you outfit it. It remains the one universal trait I've seen in those who excel in the corporate world.

Communication is the wind. It can drive your success. But never forget that real communication is much more than the capacity to speak. The greatest communicators are phenomenal listeners—and they've parlayed the magic of the audience engagement they create—along with compelling stories—into an art form.

Leadership is the fuel. It is the hallmark of truly great companies and a core skill for those who thrive in business. Most confuse its principles. Remember the power of The Five. More important, build a career that ensures your answers. Brands and strategies will inevitably change. Leadership is timeless.

There is so much more that could be written, but I began this book with the hope of offering a simple guide—not a treatise.

I hope you'll use The Compass Solution to forge your own journey.

I hope your experience will be as rewarding as mine.

I hope you'll become a Whisperer for others.

And so I leave this journal with you.

Now it's up to you to decide what your story will be. Just don't limit it to simply surviving. I've watched far too many settle into a lifetime of work. I cannot imagine a worse fate. Find something that you're passionate about—that challenges you to grow. When you do, apply the lessons in this book to differentiate yourself.

The masses follow an established trail. They interpret and respond as a group. In their own minds they think it's safer there. But it's not.

Whatever magic The Compass Solution offers is in the time-tested lessons that will give you the courage to step away and forge your own path—

navigate your own journey.

I took a job in the corporate world to make a little money and to get a company car. I had no idea it would become a best friend that traveled with me down a million miles of highway, or that it would offer incredible life experiences that would change me.

I've spent a lot of years trying to pay back the debt owed, but I know it's an account that will never be completely settled. To all those individuals who have helped me by your words and actions, thank you. Maybe this book will in some way help ensure the legacy you offered me is passed on.

It's a beautiful day and the path ahead offers adventure around every bend. Keep your eyes open. Look for the precious nuggets that encourage your heart and fire your passion.

Maybe I will see you somewhere on the trail.

Good luck.

ABOUT THE AUTHOR

Tim Cole, Successful Business Leader, Author and Speaker

Tim Cole invested three plus decades in the healthcare and pharmaceutical industry—through dozens of restructures and five mergers. He held multiple leadership and senior executive positions and played a major role in the ascent of a mid-sized firm into one of the largest in the world, with direct involvement in the launch of 20 plus pharmaceutical brands—six of which became global blockbusters. He's managed thousands of people and portfolios worth billions of dollars.

Now Tim focuses his time and energy on sharing the secrets and lessons he learned in the corporate world to help others achieve sustainable, successful and fulfilling careers.

www.thecompassalliance.com   tim.cole@thecompassalliance.com

Made in the USA
Columbia, SC
26 August 2017